D1860193

WRITING THE SELF

WRITING THE SELF
A Thematic Study of Dalit Autobiographies

Bolleddu Siva Nagaiah

KALPAZ

© **Author**
All rights reserved. No part of this book cab be reproduced, stored, adapted, or transmitted in any form or by any means, electronic, mechanical, photocopying, micro-filming, recording or otherwise, translating in any language, without the prior written permission of the copyright owner and the publisher. The book is sold subject to the condition that it shall not, by way of trade or otherwise, be lent, resold, hired out, or otherwise circulated without the prior publisher's written consent in any form of binding or cover other than that in which it is published.

The views and opinions expressed in this book are of author(s) own and the facts reported by him/her them have been verified to the extent possible, and the publishers are not in any way liable for the same.

ISBN: 978-93-5128-1238
Price : ₹ 360/-

First Published, 2015

Published by

Kalpaz Publications
C-30, Satyawati Nagar,
Delhi-110052
Ph. : 9212142040
E-mail: kalpaz@hotmail.com

Printed at : G. Print Process, Delhi

Cataloging in Publication Data—DK
Courtesy: D.K. Agencies (P) Ltd. <docinfo@dkagencies.com>

Nagaiah, Bolleddu Siva, author.
Writing the self : a thematic study of dalit autobiographies / Bolleddu Siva Nagaiah.
pages cm
Includes bibliographical references and index.
ISBN 9789351281238

1. Autobiography—Dalit authors. 2. Indic literature—Dalit authors—History and criticism. 3. Dalits in literature. 4. India—In literature. I. Title.

PK2907.U56N34 2015 DDC 891.409 23

Contents

To

Jose, Thiya Gale and Maurya.

Acknowledgements

I would like to express my deepest gratitude to my research supervisor, Prof K. Purushotham, Department of English, Kakatiya University, Warangal for his authentic guidance and constant support throughout my Ph. D research under his able supervision.

Most importantly, I express my earnest sense of gratitude to my grandfather China Anjaiah (Late) and my parents whose vision made me realise the true value of education.

I am grateful to Prof K. Ratna Shiela Mani and Prof R. Saraswathi (Rtd.) and other faculty members of the department of English, Acharya Nagarjuna University (A. N. U.), Guntur for their invaluable scholarly suggestions. I thank the non-teaching staff members Uma Maheswara Rao, Rama Rao and Manikyamma for their support. I also thank all the members of the Principal office as well as the Research Cell, A. N. U. for their needful help and proper support throughout my research.

It is my privilege to offer thanks to Prof Sukumar, Prof Prasanna Sree, Dr Challapalli Swaroopa Rani, Prof

G. Aloysius, Prof Y. Chinna Rao, Joseph Macwan (Late), Omprakash Valmiki (Late) Sharankumar Limbale, Sivakami, Prof Muneer Khan, Prof Thirupathi Kumar, Dr Sathyanarayana, Dr Murali Thadi, Dr Dasari Murali Manohar and Dr J. Bheemaiah for their scholarly suggestions. I offer my sincere gratefulness to Prof Lam Prakasa Rao, Prof Brahmanandam, Prof Z. Vishnuvardhan, Samuel Gopala Rao and Dr Surya Prakasa Rao for their support and concern.

I extend my since thanks to N. Sudhkara Rao, Head, Department of English, TJPS PG College, Guntur; Dr J. Sudheer, Principal, Dr Ambedkar Degree College, Tenali; Medepalli Sundhara Rao, Kuraganti Koteswara Rao and my grandfathers Bolleddu Chinna Anjaiah and Bolleddu Venkateswarlu – an ex-service man, the Indian Military Service; my parents, my father-in-law Boddu Ignatius, Retired Head Master, Bishop Grassi High School, Vijayawada; my brother-in-law Boddu Francis Dass and my scholar friends: Moparthi Suresh Babu, Dr B. Venkat Rao, Dr M. Koteswara Rao, John E. Bear, N. Ratna Kanth and Ch. Murali Krishna for being with me in the hour of need. I thank D. Jaya Lakshmi for extending technical support in typing the book.

I also express thanks to the librarians and the staff of the ASRC, HCU and EFLU, Hyderabad, Samanthara Dalit Book Centre, Hyderabad and Dr B. R. Ambedkar Library, Acharya Nagarjuna University (ANU), Guntur and to the publishers of Critical Quest, Delhi for providing necessary resources and materials.

Preface

The present work, "Writing the Self: A Thematic Study of Select Dalit Autobiographies" is an attempt to examine the aspects of marginalisation, oppression, discrimination and the Dalit response in the forms of resistance and rebellion. The Dalit narratives are, especially the genre of autobiography, the manifestations of the Dalit response to their exclusion from the mainstream society, the caste-based discrimination and untouchability.

The bases of exclusion of the Dalits from the mainstream society lie in the Hindu/Brahminical ideology. Casteism is a permanently organised force and an institutionalised inequality as Antonio Gramsci and Berreman described oppression in terms of hegemony. According to Althusser, this kind of dominance is an ideology through which the dominant class is able to reproduce its class domination. Brahmins use this 'ideology of caste' as a crucial instrument to dehumanise, divide and dominate the Dalits in India.

The dominance of caste-based oppression resulted in resistance and rebellion. Foucault observes that dominance and resistance often go hand in hand. But the agents of history, that include historiography, art and literature, record the mainstream aspects of life. The history of resistance and rebellion of the Dalits did not form part of the historiography, art and literature. The aesthetic forums, which were the domains of the Brahmins, either silenced or erased the voices of Dalit protest and resistance. Yet there have been attempts to bring the Dalits into the mainstream giving voice to their silenced and erased aspects of life. There have been different stages of Dalit protest.

In the present study, the scholar made an attempt at studying Dalit autobiography and its accomplishment in establishing alternative literature to Hindu dominated literature. Select Dalit Autobiographies are chosen for this study. Sharan Kumar Limbale's *The Outcaste* (2003), Narendhra Jadav's *Outcaste* (2003), Omprakash Valmiki's *Joothan: A Dalit's Life* (2003) and Baby Kamble's *The Prisons We Broke* (2008) are the works for study and they have been critically viewed in the light of Dalit movements in modern India. The work, being thematic in nature, is divided into six chapters.

Chapter I, entitled "Contextualising Autobiography: Writing for the Community" attempts to examine autobiography and its growth in India. This chapter focuses on the emergence of Dalit literature and the influence of Phule and Ambedkar on the Dalit writers. The focus of the chapter is on how Dalit autobiography has become a successful genre in providing space for Dalits in mainstream literature.

Buddhism was the earliest form of recognising the Dalit oppression and the need for liberation. Though the resistance to the caste ideology began as soon as the caste came into existence, it is only Buddhism that gave complete confrontation to the Hindu dominance. Gautama Buddha's compassion for suffering humanity, his historic challenge to the uncivil social order made the untouchables follow Buddhism. Buddhism produced a cultural-ideological synthesis within social reality and encouraged the untouchables to think independently.

Next to Buddha, saint poets attempted at reforming the caste-based system and untouchability. The saint poets are called Bhakti movement poets. Bhakti poets like Kabir, Ravidas, Dadu Dayal and Guru Nanak represented a cultural revolt. Spiritual equality, social justice and deep sympathy for the common people are major principles of the Bhakti movement. They also stressed that God is the ultimate symbol of universal love, compassion and justice. They wished that God should stand on the side of the oppressed, the weak, and the defenseless.

Then began the first radical Dalit protest movement led by Jotirao Phule (1827-1890), who fought for the freedom of India's long-suppressed humanity. He struggled to rebuild the society on the matrix of 'equality,' 'justice' and 'reason'. Phule drew a clear line between the relation of knowledge and power. In his battle against discriminatory Brahmanism, Mahatma Phule was inspired by the egalitarian philosophy of the Buddha and Kabir. Phule believed that education was the source of emancipation and empowerment, and therefore he gave maximum importance to education. Phule's *Gulamgiri* (1873) was a revolutionary deconstruction of the Brahminical culture.

After Phule's successful contribution in eradicating the sufferings of the untouchables, Dr B.R. Ambedkar's role is indomitable and unquestionable. Dr B.R. Ambedkar stood for freedom of the Dalits. He burnt a copy of *Manusmriti* at Mahad and rejected the rules of inequality. He believed in studying 'from below' and thoroughly identified the objectives of Brahminical sacred books. He pointed out that the Hindu sacred books gave higher priority to graded inequality between different classes. They are written to complete disarmament of the shudras and the untouchables. Dr B.R. Ambedkar considered the Buddhist recognition of dignity and equality of human beings and converted himself into a Buddhist. Dr Ambedkar recognised in Buddhism an antithesis to discriminatory Brahmanism.

Before the rise of Ambedkar movement in India, there were social mobilisations in the name of 'Adi-movements.' They are basically Non-Brahman in Maharashtra and Tamil Nadu, Ad-Dharm movement in Panjab, Adi-Hindu movement Uttar Pradesh and Hyderabad, Adi-Dravida, Adi-Andhra and Adi-Karnataka movements in South India succeeded in mobilising the masses. To break the Dalit Adi-movements, Hegdewar founded the Rashtriya Swayam Sevak Sangh (RSS) in 1920 and Savarkar constructed the Hindu Mahasabha. Both RSS and Hindu Mahasabha led to the downfall of the Adi-movements. Gandhi's slogan 'Rama Rajyam' and Nehruvian 'Secularism' had also caused great destruction to Adi-movements. The fragmented Adi-movements came on to the common platform under the successful leadership of Dr B. R. Ambedkar.

Under the influence of Congress and after the death of Ambedkar, Dalit movement split into groups and some of its leaders supported Congress and the rest of them remained in the Republican Party founded by Ambedkar. By 1960s, some Dalit educated youth who had been strongly influenced by Dr Ambedkar came forward to build an organisation, with an aim of fighting against social problems and the caste system. They named it 'Dalit Panthers Movement' and it was initiated on 9 July 1972. The Dalit Panthers led a huge movement to rename Marathwada University after Ambedkar. Dalit Panthers were highly inspired by America's Black Panthers and remained a revolutionary and militant organisation of Indian Dalits.

Under the influence of Dr Ambedkar and in the light of Dalit Panther's movement in Maharashtra, Dalit writers initiated the issue of self-respect in their writings. Dalit literature played an important role in establishing social consciousness among its masses. Gradually the awareness spread across India, almost in every region, Dalit writers through their poems, short stories, novels and autobiographies started questioning the caste hierarchy and political supremacy. Implicitly and explicitly, Dr B.R. Ambedkar's influence on the emerging Dalit writers is very keen and particular. Now Dalit writers aimed at breaking the 'culture of silence' imposed on them. They started telling their stories in their own language and idiom. Now Dalit is an alternative and collective word for 'Shudras' or 'Untouchables' or 'Harijans' and a symbol of environment for change, confrontation or revolution.

Dalit literature, in all its forms and genres, presents the culture of Dalits. Dalit writers, by using their own languages and idiom, are against the dominance of Sanskrit. Among all the forms, 'Dalit Autobiography' became a successful genre in depicting the originality of Dalit life style. It transforms the experience of pain into the narrative of resistance and also the means of political assertion.

Chapter II, entitled "Denial of Education: Subverting the Monopoly" deals with the exclusion of Dalits from the domain of education. The chapter focuses on how the Dalit children are excluded from schools and colleges, and the sort of discrimination they were subjected to while pursuing education. It also focuses on how the Brahminical pedagogy made Dalit students alienated in the schools. The pedagogical aspects, which take into account the upper caste children, need to be critiqued. Exclusivist pedagogy, argued in the chapter, needs to consider the culture, language and ethos of the Dalits towards an inclusive pedagogy.

Chapter III, entitled "Experiencing Discrimination: Dalit Livid Lives" is devoted to the aspects of insults, discrimination and exclusion of the Dalits experienced in the social and religious life, public places and political space as narrated in the select Dalit autobiographies. Dalits are insulted and subjected to accept the feeling of otherness.

Chapter IV, entitled "Writing Dalit Gender: Dalit among Dalits" examines the aspect of discrimination of Dalit women in the caste system and patriarchal order. Dalit girls, for example, are exploited both by upper caste and their own caste boys. Dalit women are considered inferior to their men. Their aspirations are not recognised. Being labeled as weak and psychologically immature, Dalit women are confined to domestic activities and never allowed into the public sphere. This chapter explores how Dalit women, under the influence of Ambedkar movement, identified themselves as a strong social force and able to break the oppressive social laws.

In chapter V, "Construction of Dalit Identity: Assertion of the Self" the aspects of Dalits as a deconstructive force to de-Brahmanise the Indian history and to reconstruct the Dalit forms is addressed. Dalit narratives mediated between Dalit writers and Dalits to form into a strong group of social protest against violence. The questions of identity and self-respect made Dalits interrogate the established conventional social structures. Dalit writings in the name of self-respect attracted wide critical acclaim of readers from all over the world.

The concluding chapter presents the findings of the study. Autobiography is considered the most suitable form of personal narratives combining the personal and the public. It is argued in the chapter that the personal narratives, presented in the autobiographies, also serve as the social narratives of the Dalits. By means of the personal narratives, the writers offer political contestation of the oppressive social order.

Bolleddu Siva Nagaiah

1

Contextualising Autobiography: Writing for the Community

The introductory chapter sets out to explore the importance of Dalit autobiography and its significant move in terms of reconstructing Dalit political history through memories of struggle and experience of caste discrimination. It also examines how Dalit autobiographies mark a formidable literary alternative formulation by breaking the established norms, content and form of the mainstream autobiography. Further, the impact of Dr Ambedkar on Dalit literature and on Dalit autobiography has been examined. The chapter explores the genesis and growth of the autobiography in the Indian context without entering into the Western debates on the subject.

The practice of writing autobiography is considered an independent and respectable mode of expression. Yet it is confined mainly to a small section of people belonging to the upper caste elites. The Dalits had little or nothing to do with it. As a result, it failed to form part of the Dalit consciousness and gradually stated into a stereotyped medium of mere self-exaltation. The large majority of the Dalit population remained untouched by this practice of writing the self mainly because the elite Hindus wrote it in English, a language which only a small section of the Dalits had an opportunity to learn and write.

I

Literary means of autobiography is an account of a person's life written by himself or herself. The term autobiography appears to have been first used by Southey in 1809. Autobiography speaks not only about writers and incidents but also about their experiences. Roy Pascal defines, "Autobiography is historical in method and at the same time the representation of the self in and through its relations with the outer world."[1] It is clear that an autobiography is the true representation of the extraordinary, renowned and popular men's life, achievements and experiences. But in the case of Dalits, ordinary men and women, who do not hold any prominent position in the social history and politics write autobiographies. They keep aside the established style of writing autobiographies. Moreover, it is important to see why the 'community' is given more importance than the 'self' in the Dalit autobiographies. According to A.M. Clark, "Autobiography is not the 'annals of a man's life', but it's a 'philosophical history.'"[2]

Roy Pascal views, "Every experience is a nucleus from which energies radiate in various directions. In any worthwhile life there is a dominant direction that is not accidental; therefore ultimately the life is a sort of graph linking the experiences."[3] One should have a 'worthwhile' life to write an autobiography and such worthwhile personality should have 'great experiences' to influence vast majority of people. Further, Roy Pascal's kind of analysis denies a space for Dalit autobiographies.

In this context, the main argument contests the form, contents and notions framed around the idea of autobiography by the mainstream and elite writers. Roy Pascal opines, "The value of an autobiography depends ultimately on the quality of spirit of the writer."[4] Further, he stresses, "Good autobiography represents a new of stage self-knowledge and a new formulation of responsibility towards the self; it involves mental exploration and champ of attitude."[5]

Autobiography is a presentation of the wholeness of personal identity in only a particular work and 'self knowledge' is then a primary motive of any autobiography. Understanding an autobiography is to know the psychological insight of the writer. Roy Pascal considers Susanne Langer's definition of autobiography, "Autobiography is the achievement of art which explores the intuitive knowledge of some unique experience."[6] It is understood from Pascal's argument that true autobiography can be written only by men and women pledged to their innermost selves...beyond fastened truth, beyond the 'likeness', the autobiography has to give that unique truth of life as it is seen from inside, and in this respect it has not submitted or rival.[7]

II

In the Indian literary context, autobiography as an area of academic study has not been widely debated as much as other literary genres like novel, poetry and drama. M.K. Naik in *A History of Indian English Literature* (1982) categorised the Indian autobiographies into different groups. Firstly, he gives a list of the autobiographies belonging to the pre-independence time. They include D.K. Karve's Looking Back (1936) and N.C. Banerji's *At the Cross-Roads* (1950), both of which are known as the autobiographies of public men.

Autobiographies by revolutionary thinkers include Barindrakumari Ghose's *The Tale of My Exile* (1928), B. K. Sinha's *In Andamans: The Indian Bastille* (1939), and General Mohan Singh's *Leaves from My Diary* (1946). The earliest autobiographies are Dhan Gopal Mukerji's *Caste and Outcaste* (1923), which describes his nostalgic recollections of his boyhood in India and his visit to Japan and sojourn in the United States of America.

M.K. Naik further gives a list of the autobiographies written by Hindu philosophers, scientists and other noble men, which include, Swami Ramdas' *In Quest of God, (*1923), Purohit Swami's *An Indian Monk, (*1932) and Sitanath Tattvabhushan's *Autobiography, (*1942); *Life and Experiences of a Bengali Chemist (*1932), P.C. Ray's *Autobiography, (*1958), G.K. Chettur's *The Last Enchantment, (*1933), Bhola Singh's *How to Climb the Service Ladder, (*1933), and a jurist Chimanlal Setalwad's *Recollections and Reflections : An Autobiography, (*1946) are some of the pre-independence autobiographies.[8]

The number of autobiographies by men in politics and public life is very large. These include: Mirza Ismail's *My Public Life* (1954), M.R. Jayakar's *The Story of My Life* (1958), N.G. Ranga's *Fight for Freedom* (1968), A.K. Gopalan's *In the Cause of the People* (1973), Morarji Desai's *The Story of My Life* (Vols. I-III, 1974, 1979), A.S.R. Chad's *Memoirs of an Un-repentent Communist* (1975), C.D. Deshmukh's *The Course of My Life* (1975), V.V. Giri's *My Life and Times* (1976), Goan freedom-fighter Telo de Mascarenhas's *When the Mango-Trees Blossomed* (1976), M.R. Masani's *Bliss Was in That Dawn* (1977), K.M. Panikkar's *Autobiography* (1978) and M. Hidayatullah's *My Own Boswell* (1980). Hiren Mukerji's *Portrait of Parliament: Reflections and Recollections 1956-77* (1977).

Further Naik enlists the autobiographies by eminent jurists. They are: M.C. Mahajan's *Looking Back* (1963); M.C. Setalwad's *My Life: Law and Other Things* (1971); M.C. Chagla's *Roses in December* (1973). R.V.M.G. Ramarau, Prince of Pithapuram's *Of Men, Matters and Me* (1961).

Naik also records the significant autobiographies written by women writers. They are: Vijayalakshmi Pandit's *So I became a Minister and Prison Days (*1936). Krishna Huthee Singh's *With No Regrets* (1944) and *We Nehrus* (1968), the Maharani of Cooch Behar, Sunity Devi's *The Autobiography of an Indian Princess* (1921), Cornelia Sorabji's *Whose India Calling* (1935) and *India Recalled* (1936), novelist Santha Rama Rau's *Home to India (*1945), and *Gifts of Passage,* (1961) and a Khoja Muslim Isvani's, *The Brocaded Sari* (1946—also published under the title, *Girl in Bombay,* London, 1947).[9] All these autobiographies are published before the Independence.

Other autobiographies written by women include Savitri Devi Nanda's *A City of Two Gateways* (1950)—a picture of childhood in a Punjabi aristocratic family, Brinda Manarani of Kapurthala's *The Story of an Indian Princess* (1953)—a saga of high life and not so high a sexual code, Nayantara Sahgal's, whose *Prison and Chocolate Cake* (1954) and *From Fear Set Free* (1961) are the studies of the Nehru family. Sita Rathnamal's *Beyond the Jungle (1968)*— a fascinating account of tribal life seen through the eyes of an insider turned outsider, Kamala Dongerkery's *On the Wings of Time,* (1968), Kamala Dass' *My Story* (1976), Maharani of Jaipur, Gayatri Devi's *A Princess Remembers, (*1976), and Lady Dhanvanthi Rama Rau's (mother of the novelist Santha Rama Rau) *An Inheritance* (1978) reveals how a modern Indian woman can imbibe the best in the West without sacrificing her oriental inheritance; and Durgabai Deshmukh's *Chintamani and I* (1980) is a fascinating account of the career of one of the most distinguished couple in modern India.

In fact, it could be noticed that all these autobiographies are written by well-known Indians within the prescribed style, content and form of the genre. Though caste plays a kernel role in the Indian context, there is no mention of caste in these accomplished autobiographies. The success or failure of an individual is determined by one's caste. Yet caste has been completely absent in those autobiographies. No writer has 'truthfully' represented his/her experience and encounter with the 'other' community. This applies to socially and politically conscious figures like Gandhi and Nehru, who are no exception in terms of either trivialising the caste or deliberately overlooking it. Moreover, Gandhi has romanticised his upper caste prestige and prejudice. He foregrounded his caste history and tried to show that he hailed from a baniya (business) community. Apart from his caste dominance he has revived the Hinduism and has strongly established the modern paradigm of Hindu nationalism through his political activities.

One cannot easily overlook the fact that Gandhi provided the ideological impetus to the present day Hindutva ideology. Scholars such as Gauri Viswanathan and Lancy Lobo point out that "Gandhi's approach and the [present] Hindutva approach have much in common as both of them stem from the same religious roots."[10] The ideological as well as the punitive aggression of the Hindutva forces such as BJP, VHP, RSS, Shiv Sena, Ramnirmana Sena and Bajrang Dal cannot be attributed to their obvious ideologues like Tilak and Savarkar alone. Gandhi has vehemently opposed and contorted Dalits' interests. For instance, Dalits were pursuing the conversion as one of the social emancipations. But Gandhi was against the conversions as he wrote in *My Experiments with Truth*:

> When I was a youth, I remember a Hindu having become a convert to Christianity. The whole town understood that the initiation took the shape of this well-bred Hindu partaking of beef and brandy in the name of Jesus Christ. These things got on my nerves.

Gandhi reinforces his view:

> I developed a sort of dislike for Christianity. And for a reason, in those days Christian missionaries used to stand in a corner near high school and hold forth, pouring abuse on Hindus and their gods. I could not endure this... I heard of a well known Hindu having been converted to Christianity. It was the talk of the town that, when he was baptized. He had to eat beef and drink liquor, that he also had to change his clothes, and that thenceforth he began to go about in European costume...Surely, thought I, a religion that compelled one to eat beef, drink liquor, and change one's own clothes did not deserve the name. I also heard that the new convert had already begun abusing the religion of his ancestors, their customs and their country. All these things created in me a dislike for Christianity.[11]

Gandhi's views exemplify the orthodox Brahminical world. There is no taboo of eating beef and drinking liquor or changing the dress by the Dalits. From Raja Ram Mohan Roy to Gandhi, the agenda of their autobiographies has been to redefine the Hinduism with modern face so as to reinforced the caste.

M.K Naik's traces only one autobiography, Hazari's *An Indian Out-caste: The Autobiography of an Untouchable* (1951), the first Dalit autobiography written by, the pseudonym of Marcus Abraham Malik. He was the first man from the depressed classes to write an autobiography."[12]

It is important, in this context, to briefly review some of the extracts from Hazari's autobiography which negates Gandhian perspective of caste and conversion completely. Hazari's *An Indian Out-caste: The Autobiography of an Untouchable* (1951) broke the mainstream trends in terms of language, content and conception. This is the story of the struggles of a deeply sensitive and ambitious person belonging to the lowest stratum of the Indian Hindu society. Fortunately he was engaged by one English family as a servant. From them he received kind and affectionate treatment which he would never dare to dream of getting from an upper caste Indian Hindu, "...An Indian would give one anna and think he was giving a fortune, the Anglo-Indian two annas and think it sheer robbery, while the British Tommy would give four annas and still think he had not given enough..."[13]

On the suggestion of his well-wishers, Hazari began to attend a school. It was a great thing for him to carry books under his arm every morning as he had watched other children do. He encounters with his fellow students and yet, he is pushed into thinking deeply about the reasons for the caste discrimination. Hazari writes:

> Yet my inner consciousness was never at rest and the perpetual conflict within me was something of which I could not speak to anyone. In play with other children, I was happy only to a certain point, because I knew it was only make believe, and that my real life was quite different to that of my school fellows. They had something which I wanted not only for myself but for my family and my community.[14]

An interesting phenomenon is that Hazari was taken into the service of Mr Newman, a teacher at the Aligarh

Muslim University. Both Mr Newman and the Muslim community of Aligarh played a decisive role in his life. Mr Newman encouraged him in his studies while the Muslim community gave him his long-cherished footing in society on the basis of equality and fraternity. Hence, his conversion to Islam became inevitable. Hazari writes, "I felt very happy to know that in spite of my caste I was held in high esteem; a friendly handshake from people of high rank and caste meant so much to me."[15] In exposing the hollowness of society, he is restrained but convincing. As a waiter in a hotel he had an opportunity to see people in their true colour:

> I knew the Mohammedans who came to drink and eat pastries made with lard, and I knew also the Hindus who relished a cold beef sandwich with their drink. I knew those women who came to wait for their lovers. I knew the foolish young Indians who came with women of doubtful character.[16]

M.K. Naik views that Hazari's autobiography has broken the long lasting silence in terms of Dalit representation. In fact, the argument is that Hazari's experience of life is not like that of Gandhi. Hazari had observed and experienced the caste discrimination throughout his life as a student and as a servant. Caste is a central issue in his life whereas it has never been a serious issue to Gandhi. Gandhi took a strategic move on caste issue but it is the everyday experience of Dalits. That is the basic difference between the perspectives of Dalits and upper caste elite.

According to K. Satya Narayana's argument Dr Ambedkar's *Waiting for Visa*, published after his death, is also considered the first Dalit autobiography. He says that it may not be out of place to know what R.C.P. Sinha's views regarding the matter:

> R.C.P. Sinha, a scholar on Indian autobiographies in English describes an *Indian Outcaste: The Autobiography of an Untouchable* (1951) as the, first autobiography of an untouchable known as Hazari. This autobiography is the story of the struggles of an untouchable in the early decades of 20th century. It was written in 1930s but was published very late in 1951 (R.C.P Sinha, p. 71). Dr B.R. Ambedkar, the leader of Dalits, wrote six autobiographical 'illustrations', as Ambedkar refers to them, titled "Waiting for Visa" which was published after his death. (Vasant Moon, pp. 665-71) He discusses some of 'the events' in his life in order to bring the oppression of untouchability into public, to the notice of the foreigners. Scholars have indicated that these six autobiographical extracts might have been written between 1946-47.[17]

There is a wide gap between the perspectives of Dalit autobiography and the mainstream autobiography. Dalit movement has influenced the Dalit literature. The Dalit autobiography is one of the successful genres of Dalit literatures.

III

The driving force behind contemporary Dalit literature is the thought of Dr B.R. Ambedkar. According to Nimbalkar, one of the contemporary Dalit writers, Dr B.R. Ambedkar is the source of inspiration:

> The immense potential of Dr Ambedkar and his philosophy was not restricted to himself or any one particular individual. He handed over to them the flares of his philosophy for development...His thoughts contained a graph of the progress of the people at the grass roots of the society. For this, Dr Ambedkar's life itself had become a revolution. This

> revolution had changed the consciousness of the Dalits...That is why, Ambedkar and his philosophy is the source of Dalit literature. The roots of new consciousness can be traced in the thoughts of Buddha.[18]

Dalit literature fulfills the leftover social responsibilities of Lord Buddha, Mahatma Phule and B.R. Ambedkar. It targets to sham the hierarchy in the name of caste, tribe and gender and it is always in rescue of the depressed people. Eleanor Zelliot, a human rights activist compares the Dalit Panthers' movement in Maharashtra with the Black movements of American Black Panthers. She writes:

> In the early 1970s, two Maharashtrian movements achieved enough prominence to be noticed by the English language press the Dalit Panthers and Dalit literature. By substituting the word "Black" for "Dalit" the reader can immediately understand that a phenomenon comparable to the American Black Panthers and Black literature has surfaced among the lower castes in social and literary affairs in western India. Like the American movements, the Dalit Panthers and the Dalit School of Literature represent a new level of pride, militancy and sophisticated creativity...There is in the word itself an inherent denial of pollution, karma, and justified caste hierarchy.[19]

Many thinkers, literary analysts and critics defined Dalit literature and its nature. Baburao Bagul, an eminent Dalit writer, opines that, "Dalit means one who wants to destroy the system of Varna the society along with its complete thought base...Dalit means one who wants to restructure this world and life...Dalit means one whose hands in this age have been made intelligent and transformable and for whom all weapons and sciences have been made available."[20]

The function of Dalit literature is to get rid of rotten customs and traditions and by the acceptance of new values of life, create literature having affinity with life. Baburao Bagul also opines that Dr Ambedkar is the inspiration behind the Dalit movement in India. He states:

> With these utterances I recalled the life of Dr Babasaheb was highly qualified. But his peon on learning his caste threw away his files and saved his religion from being defiled by the breeze blowing across him...Dr Babasaheb was the brain behind Mahad Liberation Movement...It was giving birth to a great war and to a Buddha, and to a great movement and thus Babasaheb created history...Babasaheb had changed his religion. As a result, Buddhism which became a forgotten religion since the thirteen century became the religion of thousands of his followers...[21]

Another critic G.B. Sardar analyses the relevance of the thought of Ambedkar and its influence on the emerging Dalit writers. In his words:

> Dr Ambedkar's movement revitalised Dalit community and turned it towards self-respect. Forgetting their suffering, they got the inspiration to struggle for their natural rights from this movement...The new poets amongst them declared through each and every word a resolve by saying 'today we see in each and every hut a full sun'. 'They said no to the dark death like life and marched forward through their writing towards bright life.[22]

Arjun Dangle states that studying Dalit literature and its role from only a literary or an academic point of view fails to present a complete perspective in assessing it. It must be assessed in the sociological framework.[23] Dangle states further:

While both Gautama Buddha and Mahatma Phule revolted against the unjust class structure and while it is true their teachings and ideas are inspiring even today a historical and objective examination of the situation reveals that it was Dr Ambedkar who was the enabling factor in Dalit literature because of his ideas outlook towards life and his struggle to achieve what he felt just.[24]

To Dangle, a famous critic on Dalit literature and known for his polemical book *Poisoned Bread* (1992), Ambedkar shaped the tradition of revolutionary thinking of almost a generation of Dalits. The literary manifestation of the social awareness is Dalit literature. Om Prakash Valmiki writes, "Dalit writers should write autobiographies so that not only our history will stay alive but also our true portrayals of wrong doers. Dalit autobiography will provide inspiration to our future generations."[25]

IV

The autobiography became an important channel to reach the Dalit communities. It reflects the self of the community on the whole. Susie Tharu considers that the Dalit autobiography is the biography of its community.[26] Dalit autobiographies are considered as the literary forms of social protest and practices. Sarah Beth gives some insightful comments on Dalit autobiography in Hindi. She states that "Dalit autobiography transforms an experience of pain into a narrative of resistance. Dalits have used autobiography as a means of assertion against untouchability."[27] She observes that Dalit autobiography contests both the basis of caste-discrimination as well as the institutional claim that caste no longer functions as a social force in modern India. It can be understood that Dalit autobiographies contextualise within certain larger socio-historical processes. This suggests as to why autobiography became an important genre, and why Dalit writers articulate this specific narrative agenda.

Sarah Beth considers that Dalit autobiography has given the Dalit writers a way of uniting with a larger 'Dalit community to create a powerful group which can be used to fight against caste discrimination.

Dalit autobiographies represent life-stories of the Dalits where the 'ordinary' or 'representative' Dalit individuals use their narratives to raise their voices for those who are silenced by caste oppression for generations together. Hence the construction of subjectivity in Dalit autobiography reflects its writer's desire to re-establishing links with the Dalit community. It is in this sense that Dalit narratives will be viewed as a means for writers to re-establish a feeling to connection to a community. Through the process of narrating their life-story with a focus on their Dalit identity, Dalit writers are able to form a powerful group which can then assert itself against the main obstacles they still face.

Dalit writers emphasise the 'experience of discrimination' and 'Dalit identity' as two necessary criteria for both writing and critiquing Dalit autobiography. Kancha Illaiah views in his polemical work *Why I am not a Hindu* (1996) that narratives of personal experiences are the best contexts that enables to compare and contrast the social forms and personal experiences. He further argues, "This method of examining socio-cultural and economic history is central to the social sciences; significantly, the method of narrating and deconstructing experiences has been used by feminists. Further, Indian Dalit-Bahujan thinkers like Mahatma Phule, Ambedkar and Periyar Ramaswami Naicker have also used this method. Instead of depending on Western methods, Phule, Ambedkar and

Periyar spoke and wrote on the day-to-day experiences of the Dalit-Bahujan castes."[28] Ilaiah further argues that writing personal narratives is possible and indeed the most authentic way in which the deconstruction and reconstruction of history can take place.

Sara Beth writes, "Dalit autobiographers also negotiate the issue of authority to represent the Dalit community by presenting their autobiography not as a result of their desire for personal recognition, but as a response to the requests from the Dalit community for representation."[29] Autobiography serves as a means for Dalit writers to reclaim narrative authority over the construction of the Dalit itself. While dominant Indian society has identified Dalits as 'inferior' and 'polluted,' Dalit writers through their autobiographies re-write selfhood in their description of their life and the life of their community.

Watching the community continually oppressed by the upper castes, the protagonist of the Dalit autobiography does not experience his pain passively, but rather pain incites him to unite with his community in a fight against caste discrimination. The autobiography serves the additional function of re-affirming and strengthening the link between the individual Dalit writer and the larger Dalit community. Sarah Beth argues "Dalit autobiography is considered a form of political assertion for a number of reasons. Besides giving Dalit entrance into a public space through identity-based narrative authority, the autobiography provides a space for Dalit writers to regain control over the constitution and meaning of Dalit selfhood and join in a show of strength with the larger Dalit community."[30]

Arjun Dangle writes that it was firstly in Marathi that a discernible category of Dalit autobiography emerged during 1978-1986. It has to be noted that the first major leaders of the Dalit movement emerged in Maharashtra. Jotiba Phule and Ambedkar have provided inspiration and direction to the Dalit writers in Maharashtra."[31] Dangle enlists some of the remarkable Dalit autobiographies produced during Dalit Panther's movement (1972). They include Daya Pawar's *Baluta,* Lakshman Mane's *Upara,* Shankarrao Charat's *Taral Antaral,* Sharan Kumar Limbale's *Akkarmashi* and Kumud Pawde's *Antasphot.* He also points out that one can see varying facets of the Dalit movement in the Dalit autobiographies. The Dalit autobiographies succinctly explore the struggle for survival, the emotional universe of a Dalit's life, the man-woman relationship, the experience of humiliation and atrocities and the question of Dalit assertion and identity.

Dalit literature is the literature of regional protest against its counterparts. Arjun Dangle illustrates the influence of the Dalit Panthers movement on the Dalit literature. He states that between 1972 and 2000, under the influence of the Dalit Panthers movement, writers drawn from the Dalit communities of Gujarat, Karnataka, Andhra Pradesh, Orissa and Tamil Nadu began to write about caste and caste-related themes. As some Dalit autobiographies have been translated into English and French, Dalit literature in India got a momentum. He states that Dalit literature and its emergence can be traced in several other Indian languages in the 1980s and 1990s.

There has been a sudden spurt in the publication of the Dalit writings. Dalit writing is being translated and published not only in English, but in other European languages too. Three important texts: Narendra Jadhav's *Outcaste: A Memoir* in English, Sharan Kumar Limbale's *Akkarmashi,* translated from Marathi into English, and Joseph Macwan's *Angaliyat,* translated from Gujarati were published by Penguin and Oxford houses in the year 2003. Jadhav's *Outcaste,* Bama's *Karakku* (1999) and

Sangati (2004) were translated into French. It is significant to note that the Dalit writers, Bama, Jadhav and Kishore Shanthabai Kale (author of *Against All Odds,* an autobiography) were invited to *Les Belles Estrangeres* in 2002, a literary festival in France, attended by 17 other Indian writers. It needs to locate this new interest in Dalit writing in the context of the internationalisation of the caste question in the 1990s.

The new visibility of Dalits and the debate on caste in the global arena created a new interest in Dalits and their literature. The present view about Dalit literature in India is a matter of not only looking for the space to exist, survive and struggle for identity but also to reconstruct the forbidden history of the community through their oral narratives. In the process of exploring the history of suffering from caste discrimination, particularly in the realm of education, politics and gender, the important questions are re-visited in the following chapters through the autobiographies of Sharan Kumar Limbale's *The Outcaste* (2003), Narendhra Jadav's *Outcaste* (2003), Omprakash Valmiki's *Joothan* (2003) and Baby Kamble's *The Prisons We Broke* (2008).

The following chapter entitled "Denial of Education: Subverting the Monopoly" examines how the narrators and other Dalits as children in the select autobiographies experienced discrimination in terms of education at schools, colleges and other places of education. An attempt has also been made to trace the problems of pedagogy of the Brahmins and how the Brahminical pedagogy excluded the Dalit children out of the purview of education.

References

1. Roy Pascal, *Design and Truth in Autobiography*, London: Routledge & Kegan Poul, 1960, 8.
2. Clark A.M., *Autobiography*, Edinburg, 1955.

3. Roy Pascal, *Design and Truth in Autobiography*, London: Routledge & Kegan Poul, 1960, 17.

4. Roy, Pascal, 19.

5. Roy, Pascal, 183.

6. Roy, Pascal, 186.

7. Roy, Pascal, 195.

8. M.K. Nayak, *A History of Indian English Literature*, New Delhi: Sahithya Academi, 1982, 139.

9. M.K. Naik, 139.

10. Gauri Viswanathan, *Outside the Fold: Conversion, Modernity, and Belief*, New Delhi: Oxford University Press, 1998, xii.

11. M.K. Gandhi, *My Experiments with Truth,* Ahmadabad: Navajivan Publishing House, 1927, 85.

12. R.C.P. Singh, *The Indian Autobiographies*, New Delhi: S.Chand & Company Ltd, 1978, 71.

13. Hazari, *An Indian Out Caste*, London: 1951, 114.

14. Hazari, 61.

15. Hazari, 121.

16. Hazari, 104.

17. K. Satyanarayana, *Indian Writing in English; Course II*, Hyderabad: EFLU Publications, 2005, 25.

18. Woman Nimbalkar, *Dalit literature: Nature and Role*, Nagapur: Prabodhan Prakashan, 2006.

19. Gail Omvedt, *From Untouchable to Dalit: Essays on the Ambedkar Movement*, New Delhi: Manohar, 1992, 267.

20. Woman Nimbalkar, *Dalit Literature: Nature and Role*, Nagapur, Prabodhan Prakashan, 2006, 30.

21. Woman Nimbalkar, 43-44.
22. Woman Nimbalkar, 45.
23. Arjun Dangle, *Poisoned Bread*, Hyderabad: Orient Longman, 1992, 237.
24. Arjun Dangle, 237-238.
25. Omprakash Valmiki, *Joothan: A Dalit's Life*, Kolkata: Samya Publications, 2003, XXVIII.
26. Susie Tharu, *Personal Interview*, Hyderabad, EFLU, 23rd April, 2009.
27. Sarah Beth, *Dalit autobiographies in Hindi: The Transformation of Pain into Resistance*, www.sanet.lu.so./EASASpapers/4Sarah Beth.pdf, 1.
28. Kancha Illaiah, *Why I am not a Hindu*, Kolkata: Samya, 1996, xi-xii.
29. Sarah Beth, *Dalit autobiographies in Hindi: The Transformation of Pain into Resistance*, www.sanet.lu.so./EASASpapers/4Sarah Beth.pdf, 9.
30. Sarah Beth, 11.
31. Arjun Dongle, *Poisoned Bread*, Hyderabad: Orient Longman, 1992, XIV.

2

Denial of Education: Subverting the Monopoly

This chapter attempts to study how institution of the caste excluded Dalits from education. The focus of the chapter is to examine how Dalits consider education an essential tool to break the chains of caste and social exclusion. The aspect of denial of education and using education as a tool by the Dalits is illustrated through the narratives of select Dalit autobiographies.

I

The Brahmins in India built an oppressive culture through which they operated their ideological hegemony. They constituted different laws which are available only in Sanskrit language. The power structures they made are quite ambiguous. Primarily the Brahmins gave much priority to dismantle the existing culture of the Dalits.

Culture determines the language acquisition of its people because language and culture go hand in hand in terms of identity formulations. To demoralise the Dalits, the Hindus used knowledge as the manipulator. Kancha Ilaiah points out two aspects of knowledge. They are: the oppressor's knowledge and the knowledge of the oppressed. Ilaiah considers Brahma's knowledge is the oppressor's knowledge:

> The Dalitbahujans have their own knowledge, reflected in several of the ideas of the Charvakas (Dalitbahujan materialists) of the ancient period. The ancient Brahmins hegemonised their knowledge and marginalised the knowledge of the Dalitbahujan Charvakas, using the image of Brahma. Brahma, thus represented the Brahmin patriarchs, and Saraswathi represented the Brahmin women who had been turned into sexual objects.[1]

The Dalits were alienated from the knowledge system of the Brahmins. This was accomplished through Sanskrit. The Brahmins dubbed the native languages and culture as uncivilised and unacceptable. The Brahmins succeeded in establishing their power over education system in India. They successfully made education synonymous with Sanskrit language and its slokas. The Brahmins succeeded in influencing the other communities and the people through religious practices. Those who turned against their knowledge monopoly were treated as untouchables.

The Brahmins maintain their monopoly over knowledge taking the support of the rest of the communities like Kshtriyas, Vyshyas and Sudhras. This kind of exclusion is found in every aspect of the Dalit lives. The Dalits' entry into knowledge centres is completely prohibited. Uma Chakravarthy made a significant study on how knowledge is monopolised by the Brahmins: "The monopoly over knowledge in the hands of the Brahmanas and the concomitant barring of knowledge to the lowest castes...Sudras and 'untouchables' were to be severely punished for violating the ban according to the brahmanical texts. Women too were barred from knowledge, especially scared knowledge."(17)[2] The Brahmins chose education as an important area to put the Dalits under their control. Kancha Ilaiah illustrates that though the Swaraj allowed educational opportunities to Dalits, the knowledge available in the schools and colleges which are completely ruled by non-Dalits is nowhere related to Dalit culture:

> Childhood formations are important for a person-female or male-to become a full human being. But our childhoods were mutilated by constant abuse and by silence, and by a stunning silence at that. There was the conspiracy to suppress the formation of our consciousness...Even after schools were opened to us because of independence or swaraj, a word which even today I fail to understand, the school teacher was against us, the textbook language was against us. Our homes have one culture and the schools have another culture...The gap between the two was enormous. There was no way in which one resembled the other. In fact these two cultures were poles apart. (14)[3]

Caste is the major factor in education

Uma Chakravarthy argues that, "'The monopoly of the upper castes' 'scared knowledge', 'book knowledge', 'intellectual inquiries' like astronomy, were superior."[4] The lower castes, who laboured, developed and preserved the knowledge of agriculture, of plants, animals, domestic livestock, weather, soil, pests, tools used in goldsmith, fishing and hunting are not considered as skilled professionals. Even the crafts skill, one of the primitive skills of the Dalits which is also implied knowledge of the materials used like metals, wood, clay, bamboo, reed and bricks is also considered as an outsider's profession.

The denial of knowledge has been a crucial part of the ideology of the caste system and it was one of the most elementary formulations of inequality in traditional India. It is because of the traditional exclusion from learning that Dalit intellectuals choose education as a weapon to be used in the resistance to Brahmanism.[5] The Dalit intellectuals understand the politics of the non-Dalit pedagogy constructed by the Brahmins by excluding the Dalits from educational opportunities. The punishment of the Dalit heroes by the Brahmins in the so-called Indian Epics like the *Ramayana* and the *Mahabharata* made the Dalits understand the Brahminical ploy. Cutting-off the sudhra (untouchable) Sambuka's head, demanding for Ekalavy's thumb as gurudakshina to Dhronacharya, the cunning Brahmin teacher of archery and Karna's ill-fate are the true examples of the denial of knowledge to the non-Brahmins, especially to the untouchables. Uma Chakravarthy studies the cunning nature of the Brahmins and kin-brahmana who incidentally excluded the untouchables from learning knowledge and mastering the archery skills:

> Over the centuries the monopoly over knowledge that brahmana men had was not merely evident in the area of knowledge...At an early stage, the growing monopolisation of knowledge by the brahmanas may have met with some resistance...Ultimately the tension between the kshatriyas and the brahmanas was resolved to accommodate them in separate spheres: brahmana men had a monopoly over ritual knowledge and kshatriya men over the means of arms. Thus, the kin-brahmana duo, or the priest dominant caste duo, came into operation...In any case the occasional examples of those who did not conform to the codes and sought to gain knowledge or skills from which they had been barred such as Shambuka, who practiced austerities normally reserved for brahmanas, or Ekalavya, who required skills in

archery, a privilege of kshatriyas who alone had the right to bear arms, or in other words, to wield the instruments of coercion, met with severe punishment. Women too were barred from knowledge under threat of violence as the story of Gargi illustrates.[6]

Uma Chakravarthy dealt with how the Brahmins and Kshatriyas went hand in hand to get control over the untouchables. She also mentioned how women are excluded from learning knowledge. She mentions that Gargi, a women philosopher who questioned the Brahmin monopoly over knowledge is severely criticised and excluded in the name of woman's entry into public places for debating. This needs to be understood as uncivic and anti-social.

Nevertheless, the British opened the education for all sections during the late nineteenth century. Jyotirao Phule recognised the importance of education and demanded the access of it to all sections. Phule stressed the importance of women education and started a separate school for women. But the historians incidentally ignore the great contribution of Mahatma Phule and his wife Savithri Bai Phule.

All the sections of the Indian society recognised the importance of education. The upper castes fought against the domination of Brahmins in colonial employment and educational institutions. Under the banner of non-brahmin movement, the upper castes from the princely states got benefited. For instance, the upper castes such as Kammas, Velama and Reddies started their caste associations such as *Kamma Mahajana Sabha* and *Reddy Mahajana Sabha* and *Velama Mahajana Sabha* in order to get their share in educational and beauracratic institutions. The missionaries opened schools in Dalit colonies during the late nineteen century and early twentieth century for various political interests. Moreover, colonial modernity produced a space for Dalits to occupy small positions in the administration, military and various industries. This process witnessed widespread awakening of political consciousness among the lower castes and communities. Their egalitarian aspirations also produced several streams of movement against the strangehold of hierarchy, slavery and feudal exploitation. These struggles threw up a determined lot of leaders who were unrelenting critics of caste and its consequences. These anti-caste campaigners confronted the hypocritical nationalist leadership for keeping pro-equality social movements out of the 'national agenda'. Phule, Shahu Maharaj and Ambedkar in Maharashtra; Iyothee Thass and Periyar E.V. Ramaswami Naicker in Tamil Nadu; Narayana Guru, Dr Palpu, Kumaran Asan, Ayyankali and K. Ayyappan in Kerala; Bhagyareddy Varma in Andhra; Mangoo Ram and Chhotu Ram in Punjab; Acchutananda and Ram Charan in Uttar Pradesh; Hari Chanda Thakur, Guru Chanda and Jogendranath Mandal in Bengal; Sonadhar Senapathy in Assam; and many lesser-known social crusaders all mocked the patriotic pretensions of indigenous elites, and attacked the system of exploitation at every level.[7] The great contribution of the social reformers in educating Dalits is discussed in Chapter V, "Construction of Dalit Identity." They rejected the high caste culture and its tradition and tried to rebuild an egalitarian society.

Chinnaiah Jangam acknowledges, "Untouchables and other oppressed sections of Indian society gained access to modern institutions and ideas such as secular education through the initiatives of the government and the work of Christian missionaries. This was an important breakthrough in the history of these communities, since through these institutions they learned the language of rights and the means of mobilisation against oppression, inequality and exploitation."[8]

Many other factors contributed to bring about substantial consciousness among the Dalits inspiring them to participate in the contemporary socio-political movements. At the beginning of the twentieth century, two major developments induced Dalits to develop their own politics. They are: search out their history and assert their identity. The special nature of the British response to the rising Indian nationalism changed the context of Dalit resistance after 1910 and particularly after 1920s. In the Morely-Minto reforms of 1909-10, the Government of India began the process of conceding elected as opposed to merely nominated Indian representation to its Legislative Councils. But the basis of representation continued to be the interests rather than geographical units. Crucially, the British expanded the concept of interest to allow for separate electorates for Muslims. This development had a dual relevance to the untouchables. Firstly, the communal status of untouchables had been brought into direct political contention by the argument of the Muslim League that Hindu numbers were being inflated relative to Muslims through false identification of what they termed the 'degraded castes' as Hindus. And secondly, the concession of representation to Muslims established a precedent for political representation of other minorities.[9]

Apart from the awareness generated by the early Dalit leaders, Ambedkar's involvement in Indian socio-political scenario made a major mark in Dalits' lives across the country. Ambedkar gave more importance to educate the Dalits. His clarion call 'educates, organise and agitate' made an indelible impression in Dalits lives.

The Indian Constitution provides special provisions for the Dalits empowerment. Particularly, the provision of positive discrimination helped a good number of Dalits to occupy important positions in Government bodies and also a good number of educated people emerged as poets, writers, intellectuals, politicians and artists. They tried to explore the reasons behind the backwardness of their community. They all have undergone caste discrimination like Ambedkar and they also wanted to document their struggle and suffering. Interestingly, they have chosen Autobiography as a form of reconstructing Dalit history and exposing the inhuman nature of Hindu social system. The following section examines the works of Sharan Kumar Limbale, Narendra Jadav, Omprakash Valmiki and Baby Kamble to understand how they used the genre of the autobiography for reconstructing the Dalit history and exposing the evil practices of Hinduism against the Dalits.

II

Sharan Kumar Limbale is one among the most renowned Dalit writers in India. He was born on 01 June 1956. He speaks and writes in Marathi, Hindi and English. Most of his writings are in Marathi and translated into English and other languages. Limbale got his B.A. degree in English in 1978, M.A. in Marathi in 1990 and Ph.D degree in Marathi in 1996 from Shivaji University, Kolhapur. He is a good academician as well as a writer and he occupied so many positions in YCM Open University and now he is the Regional Director of the Regional centre in Pune of Y C M Open University, Nashik. He is an illustrious writer, writes mostly on the Dalit struggle and identity. He wrote forty books. He is known for poetry, short stories, including his autobiography *The Outcaste* (2004). His autobiography is written in Marathi language and translated into Hindi, Tamil, Kannada, Punjabi, Malayalam languages. *The Outcaste* caught the attention of the readers on its

English version by Santhosh Bhoomkar. Limbale got many awards and won the wider acclaim from the public for his literary talents. He is also known for the critical work, *Towards an Aesthetics of Dalit Studies* (2004). He is a member of many academic and cultural organisations and many scholars did research on his writings.

Limbale's autobiography *The Outcaste* (2003) narrates the complexities of caste system and the most shocking experience as an illegitimate son whose mother is Mahar by caste and father is Lingayat, an upper caste who does not acknowledge that Limbale was born because of his relation with his mother. In this illegitimate relationship, Limbale's educational journey is disturbed by the father figure. His autobiography raises several questions such as the role of caste system, teacher, and father figure. He begins his school experience by participating in a picnic programme. Limbale who lives in Mahar colony got excited at the thought of being out of school. He participated in the picnic. He narrates the kind of discrimination that the Mahar boys are subjected to both by the upper caste students and teachers. Limbale writes:

> The Wani and Brahmin boys played kabbadi. Being marked as Mahars we couldn't join them. So Mallya, Umbrya, Parshya, all from my caste, began to play touch-and-go. We played one kind of game while the high-caste village boys played another. The two games were played separately like two separate whirlwinds. Play over, we settled down to eat. Boys and girls from the high castes like Wani, Brahmin, Marwari, Muslim, Maratha, Teli, fishermen, goldsmiths and all the teachers, about hundred or so sat in a circle under a banyan tree. We, the Mahar boys and girls, were asked to sit under another tree. The high-caste ones said a prayer before eating, which didn't make any sense to us. (Limbale, 2)[10]

The teachers in the classroom never took any measures to create an amicable atmosphere with fellow student's community. They did not disturb the status quo of caste practice in the premises of school. The girls sat close to the teachers. They were all chatting and the Dalit students both girls and boys sat like owls watching them. The teacher asked the high-caste boys and girls to collect the leftovers on a piece of paper and give it to Dalit students. Limbale and Parshya carried the bundle of leftover food on the way back. The high-caste boys and girls were laughing and joking, but Limbale's whole attention was on the bundle. Limbale says, "Mallya carried a bundle of bhakari on his head and we, the Mahar boys, followed him excitedly like hungry vultures. At last we gathered in Girmallya's farm and opened the bundle. It contained crumbs of different kinds of food and their spicy smell filled the air. We squatted in a circle and stuffed ourselves greedily. We had never tasted food like that before. We were all really gluttonous. Our stomachs were as greedy as a beggar's sack."(3) He further narrates the pathetic conditions of his family and community life. He states, "When I got home, I told my mother all this. Like the victim of a famine she said, 'Why didn't you get at least a small portion of it for me?'"(3)

Dalit students get their education under psychological disturbances. Caste discrimination is an everyday experience for them in their life. School and educational system is no exception to this kind of discrimination. For instance, when Limbale went to school the following day, the teacher had asked the boys and girls to write an essay on the picnic. The students of the seventh form were busy in writing the essay. The teacher had asked the Mahar boys of third class also to write. Both the classes were run in the same room. While the senior boys and girls wrote swiftly, Limbale sat worrying. When the teacher noticed him, apparently doing nothing, he grew annoyed and shouted, "You, son of a bitch, come on, start writing! You like eating an ox, don't you?"(7) Limbale picked up his slate and pencil, spat on the slate, smeared it and wiped his slate with his shirt which was already dirty having been used like this so many times before. Limbale did not know how and what to write. He kept thinking of how the Mahar boys and girls had squatted in a circle under a tree in the forest, eating. He remembered the hands of high-caste boys and girls offering them their leftovers, the withered tree in whose shade they sat, the bundle of leftovers, the question his mother had asked, and the teacher calling him a son of a bitch and a beef-eater.

The major problem with the teachers is that they arrange different rows for different community. It seems that the teachers never initiated to mix different caste background students into one row. Limbale reminds us, "Our school where the pupils came from high castes like Wani and Brahmin was run in the temple of Ithoba. The girls sat in a separate section. Further down the temple hall sat boys and girls from the cobbler community and then at the entrance sat we, the Mahar boys and girls. Arjya, a Mang, never sat with us. On Saturdays, the teacher asked us to clear the floor and walls with cow dung paste."(4) Apart from dividing the students on the caste lines, the teachers make use of Dalit students for all menial works. The teacher had a particular admiration for Limbale because he was an expert in gathering dung and smearing it evenly. At home he would not do even the smallest chore, but in the school on Saturdays he was made to do this duty that was allotted to him. Limbale knows that a man from his community had to carry out such duties in the village for the high-caste people.

Limbale also states that whenever the school was held in the Marwari's mansion during the rainy days, the Mahar boys had to sit on the floor whereas the other boys sat on a raised platform which was located outside to the mansion. In the drawing room, adjoining the entrance door, the teacher taught mathematics. Mahars sat amidst the footwear flung all around them and not allowed into the core part of the class room. Limbale writes, “Babali’s chappals were beautiful. I never touched my teacher’s chappals as I was afraid of tainting their sanctity. To me his chappals were like Rama’s sandals. I was used to filthy children in the Maharwada, We hardly knew what a village actually meant as we played and grew up only in the Maharwada. Heaps of garbage, tin sheds, dogs, and pigs were our only companions. We spent most of our time on Jaganath Patil’s garbage, playing, where we found bits of waste paper and sandals.”(5)

Limbale was excited at seeing his school in his first visit. He narrates, “When I first saw our school, it was crammed with children. For the first time I saw a chair, a blackboard, a cane, and a teacher. Most of all I admired my teacher’s umbrella. My schooling started in the real sense from the third form onward.”(5) It seems that Dalit students could not see any kind of affection or faith in teachers. Therefore they do not hold much respect for the teachers like mainstream students.

Dalit students make casual remarks on teachers also. Limbale writes, “We saw him. We used to shout, Teacher, ‘Teacher how big you are? The boys have run away so hold your cock.’ saying which we ran away.”(6) The more Limbale grew, the more he realised that caste discrimination was everywhere. The teacher decided to enroll his name in the register. When the teacher was convinced that Limbale was serious about his schooling, he asked Limbale his father’s name. Limbale says that “I did not know my father’s name. Strange that I too could have a father!”(45) Limbale started attending school regularly. The teacher, Bhosale by name, would sarcastically call him the Patil of Baslegaon knowing that Limbale was an off-spring of the Patil of Baslegaon. Limbale felt good as well as bad to be called Patil.

The name of Hanmantha Limbale, the Patil of Baslegaon, was added to Limbale's name in the school record. When Hanmantha, who is an illegitimate father of Limbale, came to know this, he arrived with four or five rowdies to school. His relatives too joined him and they all went to the headmaster. Hanmantha tried to bribe the headmaster by offering him a hundred rupees. In those days the salary of a teacher was only seventy rupees a month. Next he threatened the headmaster at gun point. But Bhosale, the headmaster, was an upright man. He did not yield either to bribery or to threats. The teacher said boldly, "The mother of this boy will say who the father is, and I will register only that name in the record."(45) There was a quarrel between the teacher and Hanmantha. Hanmantha applied all his tricks desperately to avoid his name as the father of Limbale and even pleaded the teacher. Finally he had gone away unsuccessful. Hanmantha deliberately denies that he is the father of Limbale. Limbale felt that his studies would suffer because of the identity crisis.

Limbale got an opportunity to escape from the stigma of being an illegitimate son. As the school in his village had classes only up to the seventh form, Limbale had to go to a high school in the neighbouring village, Chungi. Mahar students were supposed to apply for a freeship [scholarship] when they reached high school studies. To avail the scholarship, Limbale put an application form which was to be signed by their parents and the village Sarpanch. Limbale narrates:

> All this while whenever it was required, I used to put my own thumb impression in place of my parent's

> signature. Getting the signature of the Sarpanch was always a problem. Also, all this while, I had named my mother as my guardian because Masamai was not married to Hanmantha, and I couldn't very well enter his name, though I was born of their relationship…This is almost a tradition—a Patil, always a big landowner, has Dalit woman as his whore.(58)

Limbale never wanted Hanmantha Limbale's name as his guardian in the official record. Because Hanmantha had deserted Masamai for the last eight or ten years. Limbale knew that Masamai remained a keep of another Patil. He worries for the sort of life she had been living, mortgaging herself to one owner after another and being used as a commodity. Limbale feels that her life has been nothing but the tyranny of sex. When the Sarpanch refused to sign on the application form of Limbale, he felt humiliated. He expresses, "I too was a human being. What else did I have except a human body? But a man is recognised in this world by his religion, caste, or his father. I had neither a father's name, nor any religion, nor a caste. I had no inherited identity at all."(59) The Sarpanch finally signed on Limbale's freeship application because of Bhosale guruji, the school teacher and he was annoyed at what had happened.

The following day while submitting his application form, the class teacher asked Limbale, "Don't you have a father?" And Limbale replied, 'He is dead.'

The teacher asked next, 'What about your mother?'

Limbale replied, 'She too is dead.'

Listening to Limbale's answer, the boys from his village, who knew it wasn't true, stared at him like vultures. He writes, "The classroom fell dead silent like the calm after a big storm. But I was swinging like a snapped kite in the storm that went on tossing in my mind."(60) This incident depicts Limbale's helpless condition that made him adamant of the caste system that prevails only in India.

Limbale completed his high school education at Chungi and Chapalgaon. He travelled daily to Chungi from his village but he was sent to a boarding school at Chapalgaon because he had often played truant from the school at Chungi. Skipping school was not possible at Chapalgaon. He was no longer pampered as he had been at home. He had to stay with other boys from different places.

When he shifted to the boarding school at Chapalgaon all those impressions faded slowly. There were several Dalit boys around him all the time. He used to practice Hindu rituals at home but after joining in Chapalgaon boarding school, Buddhism began to cast its spell on him. There was a scope for him to explore his individual talent. He views, "I couldn't do anything much while at Chapalgaon except study. While my love for maths and drawing ended, my English improved. I was one of the intelligent boys in my class and moved with the brighter students most of the time."(81) He states that he got through the final school examination with a first class and stood second in his class. Mallya, Shirole, and Limbale had passed with merit and were greatly admired. Limbale stands out as one of the most brilliant students among the students of the school.

As he had completed his high school studies, he had to earn some money for college days. In the process of borrowing money from different persons, he had experienced humiliation and insults. Santamai, Limbale's grandmother with all her curiosity to see

Limbale must be educated begged every one for help but in vain. For an incident, he writes:

> Santamai and I went to a moneylender. He was drunk. Santamai and I stood at some distance from him. Santamai's blouse was torn exposing her breast. The moneylender kept staring at the peeping breast, but he refused to lend us the money. His look spread like poison in my heart. I wished that the blouse of this moneylender's mother or sister was torn so that I could stare at *their* breasts. I burned within. Our poverty was detestable. I wanted to rebel against such humiliation. (82)

He went to Sholapur for his college education and got admission in Dayanand College. After the school in his village, he felt free in new environment. This new atmosphere was encouraging and it made him enthusiastic. He felt that the urban atmosphere was free from caste. But his enthusiasm remained short-lived. There was a clerk in Dayanand College by name Nimbale. He was there at the counter at the time of Limbale's admission. Entering Limbale's name in the college records, the clerk asked for Limbale's caste and religion. Limbale replied that he was a Hindu Mahar. The clerk asked in surprise if there was Limbale among the Mahar as well. Because, the clerk suspected that Limbale was a Patil's name and how it would be of Sharan Kumar Limbale, a Mahar boy. To avoid further discussion over his caste, Limbale said yes and walked away. Limbale writes, "I was afraid of my caste because I couldn't claim my father's caste and religion. In a sense I was not a Mahar, because high-caste blood ran in my body. Could I drain this blood out of my body? My own body nauseated me. The agony I lived through is my own as much as that of my village. The life of my village was mine. I was wounded by this landlord's mansion."(82)

While studying in college, he was growing amidst a conflagration. The roots of the Dalit Panther's Movement were settling more firmly. Dalits were awakening under a new consciousness which became more pervasive day by day.

Friendship takes place along caste lines. Mallya, Dupargude, Dolare, and Limbale were room-mates. They were all Dalit who entered the college together with seventy generations of utter poverty behind them. Mallya had a maternal uncle, Nivruti, who worked in the post office and he gave Mallya his old clothes. Mallya gave Limbale a pair of trousers and a shirt from that lot. They had these clothes altered by a street tailor. After alteration, the clothes had two creases, one the original, the other which appeared after the clothes were altered. Both the creases were visible and made them look rather odd. But they had to use those clothes as they covered their nakedness at least.

All the boys in Limbale's hostel were Dalits. It was more or less like a camp. Dalit students were awed by their great struggle. Limbale stopped saying 'namaskar' and started saying 'Jai Bhim' instead. He substituted 'Babasaheb' for Ambedkar since it sounded less formal and more respectful. His youth had assumed a new meaning and significance. The blood flowed like hot lava through his body.

Limbale's *The Outcaste* (2003) stands as an example for picturing how Limbale and other Dalit students were denied from educational opportunities and the humiliation they went under throughout their career. It also represents how the philosophy of Phule and Ambedkar helped them to design their characters and how Dalit Panther's Movement filled their minds with true Dalit spirit.

III

Narendra Jadhav, currently serving as a Member, Planning Commission, is known for his personal narrative *Outcaste: A Memoir* (2003) in which he narrates the story of his family and of himself by invoking his identity as a Dalit. The main character, Damu is an illiterate, ordinary Dalit but refuses to be defined by his low caste identity and sub-human traditions. He asserts his human dignity and runs away to Mumbai for freedom. He defines himself as a Dalit through his involvement in the Dalit movement led by Ambedkar. He converts to Buddhism. Similarly, Jadhav locates himself in a global space and calls himself a Dalit. This identity can be called a Cosmopolitan Dalit identity.

Damu whom his family members called Dada once asked Jadav not to change his opinions for the sake of others. Damu's education was the one he received from life. He told Jadav that one should select one's path on interest but not by force: "All I have to say to you is this...Reach the top in whatever you do. You want to be a thief? No problem, but then, be so good at it that the world will salute at you and say, Oh, what a thief! What a crafty mind!"[11]

Damu's philosophy found a permanent place in Jadav's mind and remained a driving force behind his ambition. Damu also explained about the relevance of getting an academic degree. To him, it was like getting a driving license. He said to his son, "You get a license, and you keep on driving ...you don't just sit on it!" (205)

Damu's determination to see his children educated was due to the discrimination he and his family and community under went in Ozar, his village and Juna Wadala in Mumbai. The influence of Ambedkar who encountered the holy scripts through his western education made Damu educate his children, irrespective of all kinds of odds they experienced. Being a strong follower of Dr Ambedkar, Damu and his wife Sonu decided to give education to their children. It was because of the words of Dr Ambedkar to Damu when he attended meeting:

> After the speech was over, Dada clutched my brothers' shoulders and shoved them past everyone towards Dr Ambedkar. They were terrified...but Dr Ambedkar patted my brothers on the back, and asked my father, 'Are these your sons, Damu? Send them to school...Give them a good education ...they will surely rise to make big names.' (210)

Inspired by Ambedkar, Damu sent Janu, his eldest son to Chhabildas School in Dadar and the rest of the children were admitted to the local Port Trust School in Wadala, Mumbai. Jadav was out of experience in terms of caste when he was a school going boy as most of the teachers in Port Trust School were Dalits. He writes, "The teachers knew all children and their parents personally. There were many dangerous habits to pick up in the railway depot: alcohol, gambling, and burglaries. But our teachers watched us carefully and taught us the importance of education even in those adverse circumstances." (218)

After having lower education at Port Trust School in Wadala, Jadav joined a school in Dadar, where Jadav experienced caste discrimination:

> We had to get up early in orders to walk the two-mile distance school in Dadar...Other Wadala children who also went to Chhabildas maintained a distance from us on the pretext that we mixed with children of bootleggers and poor people. Our low caste was probably the main factor in keeping us apart. During the Ganpathi festival, when we went to their house, we would be given Prasad on our outstretched

> palms outside the door. They were careful not to touch us. Of course, some families made an exception to this practice and welcomed us to stay for the puja. (230-31)

Jadav discusses the denial of Dalits from knowledge. Jadav dealt with the alienated experience Janu, Jadav's brother had at Elphinstone College, Mumbai where Dr Ambedkar himself had studied. Jadav writes:

> Janu was not happy at Elphinstone. He felt ignored and unaccepted by other students, mostly from high caste, well-to-do families. So he took admission in the Siddharth College started by Dr Ambedkar, and was granted a government Scholarship. (231)

Jadav writes how the college atmosphere brought change in the attitude of his brother. Janu who felt alienated and ignored, was then able to take active role in debates and other co-curricular activities. Jadav writes, "Siddharth College gave Janu a new direction. He participated in debates and was a member of the mock parliament. The topic of all these writings and speeches was always Babasaheb and his Dalit movement." (231)

Though Janu was able to manage to come out of caste discrimination, that lead to the denial of education, the financial situation of his family stopped him to take part in extra-curricular activities. Being the eldest son, Janu did not stop himself to earn something to support his family. Janu joined morning college started by Ambedkar so as to take up part–time job as a clerk in the customs department.

Janu stands as an example of the achievement when he got selected for Indian Administrative Service (IAS). Both the father and the son and the entire family recollect the words of Dr Ambedkar:

> Many years ago, Babasaheb had told Dada, looking at Janu, 'Educate your son well.' Dada had obeyed Babasaheb's command and, in the process, Babasaheb's advice to his Dalit followers, 'Win the seats of respect and power' had borne fruit. (233)

Jadav's *Outcaste* explores the world Jadav and his family lived and struggled in. Outcaste is the success story of a Dalit family who started their life journey from nothingness, and achieved everything. They confess that the philosophy of Ambedkar was the cause of the success. Janu's success as an IAS, Dina's successful career as a boxer and Jadav's position as a successful economist and administrator are the examples of accomplishment.

IV

Like other Dalit autobiographies, Omprakash Valmiki's *Joothan: A Dalit's Life* (1998) also reflects the self of the Dalit community. He starts his life narrative with a description of his village and the place where his community people live together but aside the upper caste dwelling place. He writes, "All the quarrels of the village would be discussed in the shape of a Round Table Conference at this same spot....The pigs wandering in narrow lanes, naked children, dogs, daily fights, this was the environment of my childhood." (Valmiki, I)[12] From such a degraded social poison Valmiki emerges as an enlighten personality through his education. He indicates that he had never felt ashamed of being a low caste person. He is concerned about the continuous persecution of his community by the upper caste Tagas:

> We did all sorts of work for the Tagas, including cleaning, agricultural work and general labour. We would often have to work without pay. Nobody dared to refuse this unpaid work for which we got neither money nor grain. Instead, we got sworn at and abused.

> They did not call us by our names. If a person were older, then he would be called 'Oe Chuhre'. If the person were younger or of the same age, then 'Abey Churhre' was used. (2)

Valmiki delineates that the practice of untouchability was so rampant that while it was acceptable to touch dogs and cats or cows and buffaloes, but not a Chuhra. The Chuhras were not seen as human. Their utility lasted until the work was done. Use them and then throw them away.

Valmiki illustrates the post-Independent era as the new era which promised equal opportunities and democratic space for Dalits. He says that "the country had become independent eight years ago. Gandhiji's uplifting of the untouchables was resounding everywhere although the doors of the government schools had begun to open for untouchables; the mentality of the ordinary people had not challenged much. I had to sit away from the others in the class, that too on the floor. The mat ran out before reaching the spot I sat on. Sometimes I would have to sit way behind everybody, right near the door. And the letters on the board from there seemed faded." (2-3)

He writes about the upper caste children's aggressive mentality:

> The children of the Tyagis would tease me by calling me 'Chuhre ka'. Sometimes they would beat me without any reason. This was an absurd tormented life that made me introverted and irritable. If I got thirsty in school, then I had to stand near the hand-pump. The boys would beat me in any case, but the teachers also punished me. All sorts of stratagems were tried so that I would run away from the school and take up the kind of work for which I was born,

According to these perpetrators; my attempts to get schooling were unwarranted. (3)

Valmiki had only two friends in his school days: Ram Singh and Sukkhan Singh. Ram Singh was a Chamar and Sukkhan Singh was Jhinwar. The three of them studied together, grew up together, experienced the sweet and sour moments of childhood together. All the three of them were very good in their studies but their lower caste background dogged them at every stage.

The general notion is that teachers do not show any partiality and treat all the students equally. But, Valmiki's experience suggests that the teachers also discriminated him in all walks of life by practicing caste. Valmiki reminds us that "Headmaster Bishambar Singh had been replaced by Kaliram. Along with him had come another new teacher. After the arrival of these two, the three of us fell on terrible times. We would be thrashed at the slightest excuse. Ram Singh would escape once in a while, but Sukkhan Singh and I got beaten almost daily. I was very weak and skinny those days." (4) He futher narrates his bitter experience with the upper caste teachers:

> One day the headmaster Kaliram called me to his room and asked: 'Abey, what is your name?'... 'Omprakash,' I answered... 'Chuhre ka?' Headmaster threw his second question at me' 'ji' ... All right... See that teak tree there? Go. Climb that tree. Break some twigs and make a broom. And sweep the whole school clean as a mirror. It is, after your family occupation...Go...get to it.' ...Obeying Headmaster's orders, I cleaned all the rooms and the verandas. Just as I was about to finish, he came to me and said, 'After you have swept the rooms, go and sweep the playground'...The other children in my class were studying and I was sweeping. Headmaster was sitting

> in his room and watching me. I was not even allowed to get a drink of water. I swept the whole day. I had never done so much work, being the pampered one among my brothers…'Abey Chuhre ke, motherfucker, where are you hiding…Your mother…As a wolf grabs a lamb by the neck, he dragged me out of the class and threw me on the ground…Each pore of my body was submerged in an abyss of anguish…(4-5)

Valmiki writes that his father and mother were his great inspiration and strength. His father happens to see the kind of menial work Valmiki is forced to do by the upper caste teachers within the premise of school which is supposed to generate knowledge. His father stopped abruptly when he saw Valmiki while sweeping the school compound. He asks: 'Who is that teacher, that progeny of Dronacharya, who forces my son to sweep?'...Valmiki has never forgotten the courage and the resilience with which his father confronted the headmaster that day. Valmiki says that "his father had all sorts of weakness, but the decisive turn that he gave my future that day has had a great impact on my personality." (6) Valmiki used to interrogate the teachers about their love towards the Hindu epics. In return, he was humiliated with caste remarks by the upper caste teachers:

> Once in school, Master Saheb was teaching the lesson on Dronacharya. He told us, almost with tears in his eyes, that Dronacharya had fed flour dissolves in water to his famished son, Ashwatthama, in lieu of milk. The whole class had responded with great emotion to this story of Dronacharya's dire poverty. This episode was penned by Vyasa, the author of the Mahabharata to highlight Drona's poverty. I had the temerity to stand up and ask Master Saheb a question afterwards. So Ashwatthama was given flour mixed in water instead of milk, but what about us who had

> to drink mar? How come we were never mentioned in any epic? Why didn't an epic poet ever write a word on our lives?... Master Saheb screamed, Darkest Kaliyuga has descended upon us so that an untouchable is daring to talk back'. The teacher ordered me to stand in the murga or rooster pose... He ordered a boy to get a long teak stick. 'Chuhre, you dare compare yourself with Dronacharya... Here, take this, I will write an epic on your body.' (23)

Valmiki was humiliated both in his school and college. He realised that the kind of caste discrimination was more rampant at the college and university. He felt that the universities are no exception in terms of practicing caste in the evaluation. Interestingly, Valmiki was exposed to know the importance of Ambedkar's life during his college days. Ambedkar was an unknown entity to him up to that time. The college library also did not have a single book on Ambedkar. Valmiki quotes the inspiration of Ambedkar on him and his writings:

> Dr Ambedkar's life-long struggle had shaken me up. I spent many days and nights in great turmoil. The restlessness inside me had increased. My stone-like silence had suddenly begun to melt. I proceeded to read all of Ambedkar's books that I found in the library. I expressed my gratitude to Hemlal. He had truly shown me a new path. (72)

Education empowered Valmiki to be part of new artistic skill. He also began to write short stories, one-act plays and to stage them. He did both acting and directing. It was the beginning of his involvement in theatre. Shri Verma Ji was well-known theatre person in Khamaria. He staged several plays under his direction. He became involved in Jabalpur's literary life. He also began to develop his own views on literature.

He was more attracted to social realism than to aestheticist and formalist types of writings. Valmiki keenly observed the caste discrimination at every walk of his life. He feels that the entire value system of the Brahmins is based on lies and deception, "I had come to a decision. Things should be cleared up. I would face whatever happened." (96)

The relationship is no exception from caste discriminatory factor. Valmiki explains his love relation with Savita, a Brahmin girl who fell in love with him without knowing his caste. He also loved her truly. But he could not digest when he observes her practicing and supporting the caste discrimination in her encounter with Dalits and Muslims. Caste can become a hurdle to love between Dalit and upper caste teenagers as in the following conversation:

> 'You had given him tea in a different cup?'
>
> 'Yes, the SCs and the Muslims who come to our house, we keep their dishes separate,' Savita replied evenly.
>
> 'Do you think this discrimination is right?' I asked, she felt the sharp edge in my voice now.
>
> 'Oh...why, are you mad? How can we feed them in the same dishes?'
>
> 'Why not? In the hotel...in the mess, everyone eats together. Then what is wrong in eating together in your home as well?' I tried to reason with her.
>
> Savita defended the discrimination as right and justified by tradition. Her arguments were infuriating me. However, I remained calm. According to her, SCs were uncultured. Dirty.
>
> I asked her, 'how many SCs do you know? What is your personal experience in this regard?'

She fell silent. Her bubbliness subsided. We kept sitting on the ledge for a while. Then I asked her, 'what do you think of me?'

'Aai and Baba praise you. They say you are very different from their preconceptions about U.P. people,' Savita cooed.

'I had asked for your opinion.'

'I like you.' She leaned on my arm.

I pushed her away and asked, 'Ok...Would you like me even if I were an SC?'

'How can you be an SC?' she laughed.

'Why not, what if I am?' I had insisted.

'You are a Brahmin,' she said with conviction.

'Who told you that?'

'Baba.'

'He is wrong. I am an SC.' I put all my energy into those words. I felt that a fire had lit inside me.

'Why do you say such things?' She said angrily.

'I am telling you the truth. I won't lie to you. I never claimed that I am a Brahmin.'

She stared at me, totally shocked. She still thought I was joking with her.

I said as plainly as I could that I was born in a Chuhra family of U.P.

Savita appeared grave. Her eyes were filled with tears and she said tearfully, 'You are lying, right?'

'No, Savi...it is the truth... you ought to know this.' I had convinced her.

> She started to cry. As though my being an SC was a crime. She sobbed for a long time. Suddenly the distance between us had increased. The hatred of thousands of years had entered our hearts. What a lie culture and civilisation are.
>
> On the way back, we were both quiet. Immersed in the uproar that was going on inside me, I could feel that the tension inside me was dissipating. As though a great burden had lifted off my chest. Crossing the railway line near the station, I said to Savita, 'this is our last meeting.' (97-98).

What one can understand from the above conversation is that the relation between Valmiki and Savita suggests that secular education alone cannot annihilate the caste system even among the educated people.

V

Baby Kamble, being Dalit woman, provides in her autobiography *The Prisons We Broke* (2008) a remarkable account of Dalit women's point of view on the importance of education. She is strongly inspired by Ambedkar's thought and philosophy on education from her childhood days. Baby's father and brother were part of Ambedkar's socio-political activities and they used to closely discuss and follow everyday activities of Ambedkar. Kamble used to take part in all those discussions. Eventually she became an Ambedkarite. She has taken a pledge to educate her community and critique the myths, superstitions and Hinduism. The mainstream students usually carry high opinion of the notions of the teacher god and Gandhi. But, these figures mean nothing in front of Ambedkar's image. She recollects the speech made by Ambedkar:

> My brothers and sisters, all you folks, including the old men, women and children who have come to Jejuri from far off places. You walked barefoot for eight to ten days to get here. While on the way, you were tired, your feet ached, you had nothing but a few stale pieces of *bhakri* to eat, yet you kept on walking and finally reached Jejuri. Why? Because you wanted to see your family deity *Khandoba*. But tell me, did *Khandoba* see you? What did he say to you? Could he see your condition? Did he see your suffering? ...What good has this god ever done to you? (Baby Kamble, 64)[13]

Baby Kamble writes how the Dalits have been asked to follow a different path after the speech delivered by Ambedkar. She states that the Dalits must educate their children. They must divert the attention of the children from god and teach them good things and send them to schools. She views that when their children begin to be educated, their condition will start improving. She mentions what Ambedkar had told the Dalits:

> Our women have had a major role in being superstitious but I'm sure they will now give up these superstitions and take a lead in educating their children. They will have the honour of being the first to take this step forward. I have full faith in you, my sisters. Go ahead, educate your children. Let all our women take this step. Discard all such customs that strengthen our ignorance. My poor dear brothers and sisters do not eat carcass. Don't clean the filth of the village. Let those who make the filth clean it up themselves. Let us teach them this lesson. This slavery, which has been imposed upon us, will not disappear easily. For that we need to bring about a revolution. (65)

Baby Kamble repeatedly illustrates the personality of Ambedkar in order to reform the community from the bondage of Hinduism. She invokes that Babasaheb's sturdy physique, his glowing youth, his fair complexion, his high forehead, and his European attire, his suit and boots—all of these impressed people to no end. She also states about the influence of Ambedkar on Dalit women. She asks the Dalits to resolve and start educating their children. One of the women who listened to Ambedkar addressed the whole gathering:

> 'Let me assure you, my sisters, what Bhimrao Ambedkar says is absolutely right. We must educate our children. We must not and will not eat dead animals. We must reform our community. Let us resolve to fight along with Ambedkar. He speaks nothing but the truth. Let's follow him to the end. That is what I say'. (65)

Interestingly, Baby Kamble suggests that her grandparents were influenced by Ambedkar, "My grandparents started repeating Ambedkar's words to every person they met. They never got tilted of repeating the things that he said. All the people who came to our house had to listen to them. Here Kamble remembers what her grand parents repeatedly told her about the speech made by Ambedkar." (66)

Baby Kamble, who is strongly influenced by Ambedkar's ideology from her childhood suggests that there have been a good number of people who are influenced by Ambedkar's ideology like her. She writes:

> So many young activists, under the influence of Babasaheb's ideas, started enrolling their children in schools en masse. My father enrolled me school no. 2. His friends enrolled their children in the same school. We were about ten girls in the elementary school—Susheela, Hausa, Shanta Bagad, Begum, Savu, Ulka, Gulbakavali, Shaku, Asha and I. Quite a

> big group! After school, we all used to rush to the chawdi to listen to the discussions there. One newspaper or the other would invariably carry a report of Baba's speech in some public meeting. My father read out the report and people would listen attentively. None of us had seen Baba but his words were like elixir to our ears. (106)

She further says that "the revolutionary fervour of his words set our blood coursing through the veins. We felt as if we should go and shake the orthodox by the scruff of their neck. By the time we reached the fourth standard, we had sort of become grown-ups. We were then transferred from School no. 2 to School no. 5. This school was known as Bahulichi Shala. This turned all the boys into staunch supporters and soldiers of Baba. Students from other villages also started living in this boarding school."(106-07) They started studying Baba's philosophy and his writings. Baba's thinking influenced them greatly and all of them became his dedicated followers. Their unit gave them an identity and strength for the first time in their life. But, when they joined in mainstream school for their further studies they had to experience and encounter caste discrimination both from the mainstream students and teachers. Kamble states:

> Our school was predominantly high caste. A majority of girls in our class belonged to the higher castes. For the first time in their lives, they had girls like us — who could pollute them - studying with them. They treated us like lepers, as if our bodies dripped with dirty blood or as if pus oozed out of our rotten flesh. If they had to pass by us, they would cover their nose, mutter 'chee, chee', and run as if their lives were in mortal danger. (108)

The teacher allotted them a place in a corner near the door from where Dalit girls could not move till school was over for the day. The blackboard would be in another corner. Dalit girls could neither see what the teacher was writing on the board, nor could they raise their doubts in the classroom. If they went to drink at the school tap, the other girls would raise hell. But Dalit girls never listened to them. They were greatly emboldened by Baba's brave spirit. They would move together as one person. The higher caste girls would hurl taunts and abuses at them. The Mahar girls put on such airs. They have even touched the taps. Upper caste girls usually comment.

Generally, the upper caste men usually practice caste discrimination but not their women. But Kamble breaks that notion and provides that upper caste women is no exception in terms of discriminate the Dalits through caste prejudices and hierarchy. In such conditions, while upper caste women struck with patriarchal Hindu caste structure:

> They would hurl stones at us and throw dust into our eyes. Then we would get angry and attack them. Tucking up our long skirts, we would just barge into their groups like battering rams and scatter them. They would run away and those left behind would be prey in our hands. We would attack them furiously, pull their long plaits, push them to the ground, pinch their cheeks and hands, and torture them as much as we could. But we would get back all of this and more. (109)

The role of the teachers in India is objectionable from Dalit perspective. They are no exception in terms of promoting and practicing caste discrimination. The higher caste girls also got together to surround Dalit students. They would hurl insults at Dalit students and made comments: 'That Ambedkar has educated himself, that's why these dirty Mahars are showing off! That filthy

Mahar, Ambedkar, eats dead animals but look at the airs he gives himself!' The idea that students are socially and politically innocents are completely misrepresented in Indian context. They are being brought up with the family culture: culture of caste, culture of religion, culture of politics. When upper caste girls are physically unable to fight with Dalits they abuse verbally.

> In retaliation, we said, 'You shaven widows, how dare you take our Ambedkar's name! You have your own baldy, that stupid Gandhi! He has neither a shirt on his body, nor teeth in his mouth! That toothless old bugger hasn't any teeth! Ha ha ha! (109)

Baby Kamble breaks the myth that the children are innocent. She foregrounds the childhood experience and believes in terms of Indian politics and leaders. She adroitly brings the opinions of national figures like Gandhi and Ambedkar. In one morning, the higher caste girls hurled all kinds of insults and abuses at Dalit students in front of the teachers.

Baby Kamble and the remaining Dalit students did not stop themselves to give counter-attack against the upper caste students. Baby Kamble's personal narrative builds a kind of resistance against the denial of education to Dalits. Especially from gender point of view, Kamble's concern is very pertinent about questioning the knowledge monopoly of the Brahmins.

From the four autobiographies examined, it becomes evident that education has potential for the liberation of Dalits. The Dalits considered education as a critical cultural resource in the context of struggles that emerged out of contradictions generated during colonial times. The pursuit of education itself is emancipatory. The Dalits battled to gain entry to schools. The subaltern ideologies of the Dalit protest saw in education a powerful weapon that could fulfil multiple social transformatory goals. Education enables the Dalits to challenge the hierarchical structure and ideology of the Brahmanical hegemony. It raises critical social consciousness, instills new values leading to emancipation.

The following chapter, "Experiencing Discrimination: Dalit Livid Lives" deals with the aspects Dalits experiencing the social boycott at public places. The chapter examines how the Dalits were subjected to collective alienation from public life and how their culture is treated as unique.

References

1. Kancha Ilaiah, *Why I am not a Hindu*, Kolkata: Samya, 1996, 75.
2. Uma Chakravarthy, *Caste and Gender: Gendering Caste through Feminist Lens*, Calcutta: Stree, 2006, 17.
3. Kancha Ilaiah, *Why I am not a Hindu*, Kolkata: Samya, 1996, 14.
4. Uma Chakravarthy, *Caste and Gender: Gendering Caste through Feminist Lens*, Calcutta: Stree, 2006, 17.
5. Uma Chakravarthy, 21-22.
6. Uma Chakravarthy, 18.
7. Mani, Braj Ranjan, *Debrahmanishing History: Dominance and Resistance in Indian Society*, New Delhi: Manohar, 2005, 299.
8. Chinnaih, Jangam, *Dilemmas of Dalit Agendas: Political Subjugation and Self Emancipation in Telugu Country 1910-1950,* Dalit Conference, December 3-05, 2008, Philadelphia, University of Pennsylvania, 2.
9. Oliver Mendelsohn and Marika Vicziany, *The Untouchables: Subordination, Poverty and the State in Modern India,* New Delhi: Cambridge University Press, 2000, 99.

10. Limbale, Sharan Kumar, *The Outcaste,* New Delhi: Oxford, 2003, 2. (Subsequent references to this addition with page numbers are given in parentheses).

11. Jadav, Narendra, *Outcaste*: New Delhi, Oxford University Press, 2003, 204. (Subsequent references to this addition with page numbers are given in parenthesis).

12. Valmiki, Omprakash, *Joothan: Dalit's Life*, New Delhi: Samya, 2003, 1. (Subsequent references to this addition with page numbers are given in parentheses).

13. Kamble, Baby, *The Prisons We Broke*, New Delhi: Orient Longman, 2008, 64. (Subsequent references to this addition with page numbers are given in parentheses).

3

Experiencing Discrimination: Dalit Livid Lives

Caste discrimination is common among the Dalits in India. The Indian English writers addressed the issue from the nationalist and progressive point of view, which suffers from the limitations of social exclusion. The Dalit writers, contrarily, narrate the discrimination authentically. This chapter attempts to examine the experience, form and nature of discrimination as narrated in Sharan Kumar Limbale's *The Outcaste* (2003), Narendra Jadhav's *Outcaste: A Memoir* (2003), Omprakash Valmiki's *Joothan: A Dalits Life* (2003) and Baby Kamble's *The Prisons We Broke* (2008). The focus of the study is on the aspect of discrimination and humiliation. The aspect of self-respect that the authors used as the strategy to overcome the discrimination and humiliation is explored in the chapter.

I

Sharan Kumar Limbale's *The Outcaste* (2003) is about an untouchable family in general and community struggles in particular. The author narrates about how an innocent Dalit couple Kamble and Masamai are discriminated and exploited by an upper caste landlord

Hanmantha Limbale for whom the poor couple used to work day and night. Ithal Kamble, Masamai's husband is a farm worker on a yearly contract to Hanmantha Limbale and it was a job worth seven or eight hundred rupees. Ithal Kamble toiled on the farm of Hanmantha and was helped by him during hard times. Hanmantha Patil ruined the poor family and it led to the separation of Ithal Kamble and Masamai forever. After the divorce with Masamai, Kamble left the place with two sons Surya Kanth and Dharma and remarried a woman who is also a widow.

Masamai remained a keep of Hanmantha Limbale and gave birth to Sharan Kumar Limbale. Masamai was given a rented house at Akkalkot. Limbale writes, "After my birth the mansions of the Patil community must have become tense. My first breath must have threatened the morality of the world. With my first cry at birth, milk must have splashed from the breasts of every Kunti." (Limbale, 36)[1] Limbale remained like Karna in the epic, *Mahabharatha*.

Limbale states that to be born beautiful among Dalits is a curse. As Masamai was beautiful, she was lured by Hanmanth. She was made separate from her husband and suffered a lot in her post-widowed life. Though Hanmanth enjoyed the beauty of Masamai, he was self-conscious that Masamai was a Dalit and tried to avoid her. He also commented that the newborn child was looked after by Bhondya, the potter. Limbale writes, "Finally my mother and I come to stay with Santamai, my grandmother. Only a mother and the earth can accommodate and stomach everything?" (37)

The upper caste men in every village had made whores of the wives of Dalit form labourers and Masamai was one among them. After divorced from Ithal Kamble, Masamai gave birth to Sharan Kumar Limbale. Limbale's birth is the result of Masamai's private and helpless relation with Hanmantha Limbale, the village patil. After Sharan Kumar and Nagi, Masamai gave birth to many children that include, apart from Sharan Kumar and Nagi, Nirmi, Vani, Suni, Pami, Tamma, Indira and Sidramma. Limbale writes:

> We were all of one womb and blood. We shared a common mother but different fathers...I was born from her affair with Hanmantha Patil. Masamai had Nagubai, Nirmala, Vanmala, Sunanda, Pramila, Shrikant, Indira and Sidram from Kaka, whose name was Yeshwantrao Sidramappa Patil, the head of the village named Hanoor."(38)

Masamai's life speaks out how the poor Dalit families were destroyed and the innocent Dalit women were exploited. Masamai neither belonged to the Patil community as she was a Mahar woman nor a Mahar as she became a whore of Patils of different villages. Masamai and her children lived in Maharwada but without Mahar [Dalit] identity due to impurity in Limbale's blood. This kind of alienation experienced by Limbale is described throughout his autobiography.

From the day Limbale was born, he was brought up by Mahmood Dastagir Jamadar, a Muslim. Jamadar, whom Limbale called Dada had been with Santamai, Limbale's grandmother. Jamadar was Limbale's grandfather in the sense he lived with his grandmother. Limbale writes "Does this mean I am a Muslim as well? ... Who am I? To whom is my umbilical cord connected?" (38-39).

The Outcaste depicts the most humiliated events and insults Limbale and his family members underwent in different places like Akkalkot, Hanoor, Chungi, Chapalgaon, Sholapur, Ahmedpur, Barshi and

Bhimnagar in Latur. Akkalkot was a small village where Masamai was kept in a rented house. Living in Akkalkot, Masamai lost her attachment with Maharwada and lived in the conditions of adversity. Hanmantha Limbale, the Patil of Basalegaon lured Masamai but never dared to keep her in his family and always kept her in Akkalkot as she was an outsider. Hanmantha Limbale wanted Masamai's body and not her caste. Limbale writes, "Hanmantha Limbale lured Masamai. She was given a rented house at Akkalkot, which she accepted. It was a kind of revenge to live openly with the same man who had uprooted her from her family. Hanmantha Limbale possessed her like a put dove. They lived happily. Masamai became a pregnant and gave birth to a son. Who's the father of this boy? Hanmantha didn't want any of this to happen, but who can disown a child? A child is a reality." (36)

After Limbale was born, Hanmantha had been trying to avoid them and there were quarrels everyday as he did not acknowledge Limbale as his offspring. Leaving Akkalkot, Masamai went to Hanoor where Santamai, Masamai's mother was living with Jamadar, a Muslim. Sharan Kumar Limbale calls Jamadar Dada who works as a porter in Hanoor bus stand. In Hanoor, Limbale subjected to caste discrimination. When he was a school boy, all the boys and girls in the school were set out for picnic. Knowing it, Limbale felt excited and joined the group of students and teachers. After enjoying for some time at the picnic spot, all the boys and girls sat for lunch. Though they belonged to the same village, the Dalit students were not allowed to sit among the upper caste students. Limbale writes, "Even the tree we sat under was tattered like us. Whenever the wind shook it branches it produced waves of hot air that hit our faces. We sat in its broken shadow." (2) After having lunch, the teacher asked the high caste boys to collect the leftovers on a piece of paper and give it to Limbale, Malya and other Dalit children. Limbale states, "The high caste girls from our village offered us their curry and bhakari's without touching us" (3).

The following day, the teacher asked the boys and girls from first standard to seventh standard to write an essay. Limbale, being in the third farm, was unable to write anything. When the teacher noticed Limbale doing nothing, he grew annoyed and shouted, "You, son of a bitch, come on, start writing! You like eating an ox, don't you?" (4) Listening to the teacher, Limbale took his slate and pencil to write something but failed, "I didn't know how and what to write. I kept thinking of how we had squatted in a circle under a tree in the forest, eating. I remembered the hands of high caste boys and girls offering us their leftovers, the withered tree in whole shade we sat, the bundle of leftovers, the question my mother had asked, and the teacher calling me a son of a bitch and beef-eater. How should I start writing the essay my teacher had asked for?" (4)

The untouchable children were not allowed to sit in the class and asked to sit on the platform. Dalit children sat amidst the footwear flung all around them. Limbale states "During the school interval, the other boys threw stones at me and teased me calling aloud Mahar."(6)

Another experience of discrimination was at the Barbar's shop. The Barbar was immovable and not accepted to cut Limbale's hair. Limbale states, "I was a school boy, and wanted a haircut like that of other boys in the school. So, I went to the barber for the first time." (22) The barber first looked at Limbale and them at his head and shouted at Limbale not to stand there as he was not going to shave Limbale's head. Then Limbale showed the barber the money he had but the barber commented to another customer who sympathised with

Limbale that he was a Mahar so he didn't want to cut his hair. In this context, Limbale raises a question, "How could this barber, who used to shave buffaloes in the village, refuse to shave my head?" (22)

Limbale's family had no home to live. They spent most of the time inside the bus stand in Hanoor. Limbale writes:

> To us the bus stand was like home...We lay like discarded bus tickets. We had to get up early in the normally or risk annoying the driver and the conductor. Once they actually thrum our sheets and rugs out on the road? (42)

The school in Hanoor village where Limbale studied had classes only up to the seventh form. When he finished his seventh form, he had to go to a high school in the neighbouring village, Chungi. After joining the Chungi School, Limbale and other students were supposed to apply for a scholarship, and the application was to be signed by their parents and forward it to the village Sarpanch. To Limbale, getting the signature of the Sarpanch was a problem as the Sarpanch was in favour of Patil Hanmantha Limbale and said, "I don't approve the name Masamai Hanmantha Limbale?" (59) Limbale never wanted Hanmantha Limbale's name as his guardian in the official record because Hanmantha had deserted Masamai long back and she was living with the Patil of Hanoor, Yeshwantrao Sidramappa. The Sarpanch refused to sign because he was confused to decide Masamai's real husband. At this point Bhosale guruji, teacher of Hanoor School proposed Limbale's grand mother Santamai's name but the Sarpanch refused because she was living with a Muslim. Limbale writes, "The Sarpanch was in a real fix about how to identify me. But I too was a human being. What else did I have except a human body? But a man is recognised in this word by his religion, caste, or his father. I had neither a father's name, nor any religion, nor a caste. I had no inherited identity at all." (59)

In Hanoor village, God Mahadev festival was observed in the month of *Shrawan*. On that day Limbale's mother would bathe him and powder his face to make him look smart. Because Hanmantha, because of whom Limbale was born would visit Hanoor with the group of singers. Once Kaka, the present keep to Masamai brought Hanmantha, the previous keep of Masamai along to dine with Masamai and Limbale. Masamai had made egg curry for them. Both Kaka and Hanmantha were drunk and there was a fierce quarrel between Kaka and Masamai. Masamai, Limbale's mother cursed and abused Kaka and drove him out of their house. But after some time both Kaka and Hanmantha came back and the same quarrel took place among them. As a small boy Limbale did not understand what exactly went wrong between Masamai and Kaka who bought Hanmantha. Later he came to know the reason. He states, "It took quite sometime for me to know why my mother was so angry. Kaka was persuading my mother to sleep with Hanmantha." (61)

Another incident Limbale experienced is about the discrimination in religious practice. In Hanoor, there was a village temple called the temple of Ithoba in which some of the villages especially from upper castes would read Holy Scriptures. One day, Limbale and his friend Parshya entered the temple of Ithoba and prostrated directly before the God. The entire scene was watched by Parshya's father who thought that the untouchables must not enter the temple of upper caste God Ithoba and thrashed Parshya very badly stating that Parshya and Limbale polluted the God Ithoba. Limbale writes about the angry behaviour of Parshya's father, "He was angry, because entering a temple is a crime. We were supposed to say our prayers from the steps outside. Our entering of temple will make God impure. We were expected to behave responsibility. The untouchables must not enter a temple?" (62) Limbale raised certain questions like, "Why are we ostracized? Why are we kept away from other human beings? Why are we kept out of our ownselves? Why this discrimination between one human being and another? After all isn't everybody's blood red?"(62)

As Limbale was an illegal off-spring of a Patil, he was not treated as a true Mahar. Whenever Limbale wanted to sit in the community hall meant for Dalits, he was driven away stating that it was not his father's community hall, "....I did not go to the community hall for a few days. Had I gone, someone might have smacked or abused me. I am an alien ...In the Maharwada I felt humiliated as I was considered a bastard; they called me *Akkarmashi*[2]. Yet in the village I was considered Mahar teased as the offspring of one."(62)

Limbale was humiliated not only by Mahars but also by his own sisters. Whenever Nagi, one of his sisters annoyed, she abused Limbale. Limbale writes about the behaviour of Nagi with him, "you have no connection with us. Nobody knows where you come from. Our fathers are not the same."(63) Listening to there words, Limbale burned within. He writes, "Nagi's words pierced my heart. The feeling of alienation weighed heavily on my mind."(63)

Dalits were discriminated at the public places. One day when Parshya and Limbale were on their way to pluck the fruits of a toddy palm, they saw Shobhi, an upper caste girl face each other in a narrow path. Shobhi asked them to stay and let her pass. She felt authoritative in voice when Parshya argued. She said, "Mahars have become bold these days. They now dare to walk straight up to you. Can't you see I am carrying drinking water? Your touch will make it impure." (70) In this context, Shobhi's words make one understand that she worried more about the pollution of water due to facing the Dalits on road than walking with heavy pot on her head. Parshya and Limbale planned to take revenge on Shobhi. In fact they wanted to rape her. Limbale writes, "Shobhi stood before us as a symbol of the caste system. Her feet, her thighs, her arms, her face – everything was a part of the systems she belonged to."(71)

Limbale completed his high school education at Chungi and joined in boarding school at Chapalgaon. Chapalgaon was four miles away from Limbale's village, Hanoor. As majority of the boys in Chapalgaon were Dalits, Limbale slowly came to know about Buddhism which gave him sense of self-respect. One day Santamai, Limbale's grandmother walked the long distance between Hanoor and reached Chapalgaon just to see Limbale. She also brought him a pair of old chappals of someone who had forgotten them at the Hanoor bus stand. Though the chappals were of a woman, Santamai did not give them either to Nagi or Nirmi but kept for Limbale. Because Limbale used to go to school without chappals. But one of the chappals that Santamai brought was to be repaired and Limbale went to the cobbler. But the cobbler, who knew Santamai living with a Muslim, refused to repair the chappal. Limbale, unable to convince the cobbler, put the ladies chappals on his feet besides being teased by his friends at school.

Limbale became more and more conscious of caste as he reached one standard after another in studies. His studies changed his thinking. He felt that casteism made the Dalits bitter but had a sense of pride through education. Limbale could remember the caste discrimination in public places like at hotels and at the other meeting places was very severe. He writes, "Casteism made us bitter. There was a small tea shop in our village owned by Mangs, where a separate cup and saucer were kept for the Mahars and Mangs. I had seen the cup and saucer many times. We also had to move aside to make way for high-caste persons while passing on the road."(76) Dalits were condemned at every place and at every stage of life whether it is public or private. Limbale mentions:

> Our houses were in places that other villagers used as latrines. We felt no affection for our villages. Instead, we were scared and tense. Our caste had been thrust upon us even before we were born. (76)

Dalits were excluded from social life. All the provisions were denied on petty reasons like they were intentionally killing the animals of the upper caste people. Whenever the Dalits were accused of poisoning animals, the village Patils sit together to punish the Dalits and that kind of experience was meted out to the Dalits for very baseless reasons. Limbale quotes his grandmother Santamai's words how the upper caste used to punish the Dalits on the reasons of stealing and poisoning their animals:

> Whenever an animal in the village died, the villagers grew annoyed. They considered the Maharwada responsible for it. They tied us to a pole and beat us like animals. They accused of having poisoned the animal. Our women and children cried and shrieked. All the men in the Maharwada were very badly beaten. The village then ostracized the Maharwada for a few days. We would not get any work on the farms. We were decided any provision at the shops though we had the money and were ready to pay. We had reached a dead end. Such humiliation was agonizing. (78)

Water was under the control of the high castes. Though the village wells were dug and built by Dalits, they were not allowed to fetch water from the wells. One could also see why Dr Ambedkar gave stressed about the right for Dalits on water from the limitations of the upper castes. Kolakaluri Enoch, one of the distinguished Telugu Dalit writers in Andhra Pradesh states in his polemical book "*Oorabaavi*" (Public Well, 1969) how a Dalit woman had thrown skin into the well to save water from the upper caste hands. The Reddys never allowed Madigas, a Dalit sub-caste in Andhra Pradesh. To resolve the problem, a Dalit woman, with all her courage to make the Reddys disown the well, threw a dead animal's skin into the well after which the upper caste Reddys left the well. Later the Dalits cleaned the well and drew water from it. This is how Dalit women succeeded in getting water.[3] Enoch's story contains aspects like search for self-respect, the angst and language of Dalits.[4] Similarly Limbale claims, "Even the water was under the control of the high castes...What is so peculiar about our touch is that it pollutes water, food, houses, clothes, graveyards, teashops, god, religion, and even man." (81)

Limbale was honest and it was witnessed through an example he mention in his autobiography. Once Limbale found thirty rupees and handed it over to the head master. The following day when Limbale entered his class, Heremath, the class teacher praised Limbale, "This year we lost in sports, but it hardly matters. The honesty that this boy, Limbale has shown is our real victory."(75)

Whenever people were in need of help, Limbale never stopped himself to help the needy. Once Shivappa, an upper caste one was working on his farm. Limbale noticed that Shivappa's wife was carrying food in one hand and her child in the other. Shivappa's wife on seeing Limbale, she requested him to put the bundle down. Meanwhile, Shivappa who watched the scene came and shouted at his wife for seeking help from Limbale stating that he was a Mahar. Stating these words to his wife, Shivappa took off one of his shoes and threw it at Limbale. This incident suggests that the mere touch of Dalits would pollute the food of the upper caste.

Though education gives self-esteem and honour, Limbale faced severe discrimination. After passing final school examinations in first class and standing second in his class, Limbale got admission in Dayanand College, Sholapur. Limbale, though good in studies, suffered to manage money for paying the fee. Santamai, his grandmother and Limbale went to an upper caste money lender who was drunk and looked at the exposed breast out of Santamai's torn blouse. He refused to give them money. Limbale writes:

> His look spread like poison in my heart. I wished that the blouse of this money – lender's mother or sister was torn so that I could stare at their breasts. I burned with in. Our poverty was detestable. I wanted to rebel against such humiliation. (82)

Higher studies made Limbale more conscious about humiliation, discrimination that Dalits underwent. Limbale writes:

> While studying in college, I was mutually a flame. I was growing amidst a conflagration. The routs of the moment were settling more firmly. Injustice towards us was assuming a new meaning. We were awakening under a new consciousness which was becoming more pervasive day by day. (83)

Limbale reminds that Dalit students live in poverty which forced them to live with limited facilities in the hostels. Living with minimum facilities in hostels was yet another form of discrimination. Limbale writes:

> Our poverty didn't allow us to enjoy the luxuries of college life ...We continued our education amidst great poverty... There were so many Dalit students like us. This pain of poverty was not just mine. We all existed like grains crushed in a stone grinder. (83)

Limbale and Mallya were close friends who came from the same village and continued the studies up to B.A. in the same class. As they were close to each other, Limbale accompanied him. Near to Mallya's home, Janabai, another sweeper used to live. Whenever both the boys visited Mallya's grandmother, they talk to Janabai too. Later Janabai considered Limbale good at studies. She thought of arranging his marriage with her niece. Moved by the proposal, Limbale and Mallya went to see the girl. They reached Janabai's place and asked if she had brought the girl whom Limbale considered his prospective wife. When they asked to show them the girl, Janabai went wild and shouted. Limbale remembers Janabai's words, "We haven't yet lost our self-respect. Our family is of pure blood so we also expect the same of a bridegroom. Just anyone won't do for us. What does if matter however good the man is?" (88)

In another situation, Limbale was discriminated by the people of his community as he was born of illegal relations. Once, Limbale came to know that Santamai was going to ask for Mallya's sister to be Limbale's bride. Limbale was happy to marry Mallya's sister since Mallya and Limbale were classmates and more than that they were good friends from childhood. Limbale remembers his days with Mallya, "Mallya and I had been classmates right from the first standard in the village school up to B.A. We had eaten from the same plate and had drunk water from the same vessel. We had also shared the same bed." (92) But, the idea of marriage resulted in a gap between them. Limbale writes, "I was very happy at the idea of marrying the sister of such a dear friend. But the news that Sivaji brought the next day pierced my heart. Mallya's parents had refused the proposal because I was not of pure blood. These people love conventions more than they do human beings." (92) Limbale states his helplessness:

> I was terribly angry at its customs, but I was helpless. I had suffered the pain of insults. The thought of marriage was intolerable to me. The thought of selecting a girl as a match shocked me like acid thrown on me. I didn't want such shocks. It was better to stay unmarried. (92)

Choosing the brides and bridegrooms to Masamai's sons and daughters became a herculean task to her. She requested everyone who visited her house for drinking liquor. Masamai and Santamai tried hard in searching for the suitable matches to their children. Unable to select a Mahar bride to Limbale, Masamai intended to marry her son with her friend's daughter. Masamai's friend was 'Mang' by caste and had a daughter, born of her liaison with a Patil. The girl went around a singer accompanying a drummer. As no one came forward to give their daughter, Masamai and Kaka decided to select a girl as the proper match. Limbale writes:

> A bastard must always be matched with another bastard. No one else will marry their daughters to a bastard like me...at such moments. (98)

Limbale further mentions, "I remembered Maryappa, who under the influence of liquor had promised to give his daughter in marriage to me." (98) To his expectations, one day Maryappa came to Sholapur and asked Limbale to marry his daughter Kusum. Limbale accepted the proposal though he did not see her by that time. Thus, Limbale succeeded in selecting his life partner after a series of insults. Limbale's wedding was filled with great uncertainty. Masamai and Kaka wanted to follow Hindu marriage order where as Limbale's in-laws wanted do it in Buddhist way. Frustrated Limbale addressed the gathering that they were going to be wedded according to the Buddhist rituals. After the marriage, Limbale was unable to avoid disturbances and insults due to his caste and half-breed blood and Dada's religion.

After marriage Limbale's in-laws refused to send their daughter with him. Limbale's mother-in-law said that there was no discipline in his house and they left for Barsi, where they lived. Whenever Limbale went to Barsi to meet his wife, there would be a quarrel between Limbale and his in-laws. Limbale's father-in-law quarreled with him and his mother-in-law abused at him. She said, "You are rotten people. We have purified you. You were lying on the garbage." (100) Limbale was not allowed to meet his wife and whenever he went, he was asked to sleep outside. Limbale's in-laws disliked him because of his association with Dada, a Muslim by religion. One day Maryappa Kamble, Limbale's father-in-law argued with Limbale, "My son is the president of the Dalit Panthers. He is highly respected by his followers. You say that you are a relative of that Muslim. You are the cause of humiliation for us among our own caste. We have told everyone that you are of pure blood. You must have self-respect, otherwise don't enter our house." (101) At last Limbale took away his wife in spite of the possible protests from his in-laws'.

Limbale got a job as telephone operator at Ahmedpur. Due to his financial conditions, he accepted the job and gave up further education. Limbale had a new problem after marriage and finding a job. He found it difficult to find a house. Being unable to live as Dalit among the upper caste houses, Limbale said that he was a Lingayat by caste. To avoid discrimination, Limbale pretended that he was not related to Mahars:

> If I happened to see a Dalit friend approaching, I quickly altered my route. If he abruptly appeared in front of me, I greeted him with a 'Namaskar' instead of 'Jai Bhim'. Even if someone said 'Jai Bhim' to me, I responded with a namaskar. If I happened to be going with a high caste friend and someone greeted me with a 'Jai Bhim', I felt like an outsider. I was worried that my caste would be revealed. (104)

Limbale's reason for hiding his caste was that, "If they came to know my caste, they would drive me out of the house that I had rented from a high caste landlord. I would be beaten badly. They would even torture my wife."(104) Dr Ambedkar too experienced similar predicament. Though Limbale lived among the houses of the upper caste people, he was apprehensive of being identified as a Dalit.

In a particular context, Limbale's grandmother arrived to take Vani back home. She brought a bundle of beef from the village. But Limbale shut the doors and windows of his house. But Santamai said, "My boy, eat this. I know you don't get this here. Who is going to see you eat it? We will also join you."(104)

Limbale and his wife intended to take part in the birth celebrations of Dr Ambedkar. Limbale writes, "What would happen if the volunteers of this vast Dalit movement came to know that I was impure? ... I felt extremely sad about my low birth. So what about me? I am a whirlwind." (106) Later Limbale was transferred to Latur from Ahmedpur. He experienced displacement as all his friends were left at Ahmedpur. In Latur too, Limbale faced the problem of finding a house. He said that his caste followed him like an enemy. Though Latur was such a big place with huge buildings, houses and bungalows, Limbale was turned away wherever he had gone for rented house with the remarks, "We don't want to rent out our house to Muslims and Mahars."(106)

Finding that it was impossible to find a house in the town, Limbale settled in a small house in Bhimnagar, which in Latur was also the graveyard of the Marwari community. Mahars in Bhimnagar lived under tin roofs in poor and helpless conditions:

> Here the houses did not have bathrooms and toilets. Women bathed openly and urinated every where in the open. I felt awkward while walking through this locality. In the morning and evening women used to shit openly by the roadside. I felt embarrassed to walk between rows of shitting women squatting on both sides of the road. Cycle–rickshaw drivers, porters and labourers were the main inhabitants of this locality. People lived in the smallest possible spaces. Each one worried only about his hunger. The stomach was the threshold of their capability. (107)

Limbale's autobiography speaks about many uneven conditions that he experienced as an off-spring of Mahar and upper caste private relation and struggled a lot for being identifying himself as Dalit.

II

Narendra Jadav's *Outcaste: A Memoir* (2003) is a journey of finding out remedies to trespass the boundaries of caste and gender. It is comparable to Malcolm X's *Roots* and Maxim Gorky's *Mother* in which history and human relations play vital role in educating oneself. Jadav's *Outcaste* represents the struggle of the Dalits against caste discrimination, illiteracy and poverty. Having the weapons of education, empowerment and democracy, Damu, the protagonist and his wife Sonu fought for self-assertion and self-respect which are denied to them for hundreds of years. It is not the life story of Damu and Sonu; a story of all the Dalits in the world. Narendra Jadav's father Damu was inspired by Dr B.R. Ambedkar:

> Damu was not a leader...but he refused to define himself by circumstances and aimed at shaping his own destiny. Damu had no formal education...yet he steered his children to education heights and inculcated in them the spirit of excellence. Damu was not a guru...but he taught his children to believe in themselves and reclaim human dignity.
>
> Damu was often humbled...yet he maintained, 'Goats are sacrificial offerings, not lions.' Damu was an ordinary man, they said ...but he did an extraordinary thing: he stood up against the tyranny of the caste system. (Jadav, IX)[5]

Damu educated his wife and children. Damu, a young man in his twenties, worked as a *yeskar*[6]. As a yeskar, Damu's duty was to announce the arrival of the officials to the village and taking care of the guests and their horses and watch the dead bodies in the village. Once Damu went home to have some tea as he spent much time in assisting the Mamledar, a senior Revenue Official. Damu announced about the great arrival of the Mamledar:

> Damu was running as fact as he could in front of the Mamledar's tonga, heralding his arrival. Outspacing the house, he ran until he felt his legs would give way. He ran singing the praises of the Mamledar, alerting the villages that an honourable person was arriving. (3)

Damu had to wait outside the house of Patil until the Mamledar came out of Patil's home. Damu was tired and hungry by the time the Mamledar left the place and Damu walked home slowly. Scarcely had Damu reached home when a policeman came looking for him. Damu sensed that something terrible had happened. Damu was told by the constable that a dead body had been found floating in the broken well by the mangroves.

Damu who did not eat anything since morning pleaded with the constable that he would be back in no time after eating something. But the constable lifted his baton as if to strike him, "Do you see my baton?...I'll stick it up your ass and you will see it come out of your throat. I'll beat you up so badly that you'll forget the name of your father." (3) Unable to face the constable, Damu ran towards the mangroves without stopping anywhere. Mahars were not treated as human beings and they were treated as people without self-respect. Damu worried much about his wife who would not take water without some word about him and requested the constable that at least he could inform his wife that Damu could come only after the cremation of the body found in the well.

Unable to convince the constable, Damu got ready himself to the assigned duties. Narendra Jadav explains the poor condition of Damu. He said that Damu managed to keep awake, pacing up and down and drinking water to quench his hunger. He waited impatiently for the Fauzdar. The police would draw the body out, the report would be written, and the dead women would be handed over to her family. Then he could go home. He expected this to take no more than an hour or two at the most. (5)

Namya, one of Damu's cousins, came to the well bringing some bhakris. Namya told Damu that everyone especially Sonu worried about Damu all the night and gave the bhakris to Damu but Damu was not ready to eat because the constable and the Fauzdar might arrive at any moment. Even as they were talking to each other, the constable arrived. The inhuman behaviour of the constable indicates that the Mahars are not permitted to have meals, "What did they care if a Mahar liver or starved, or even died? All they were concerned about were the high-born." (6)

He came cracking his whip, having arrogant look. Damu was ordered to fetch hay and water to the Fauzdar's horse. Moving around, the Fauzdar looked into the old well which was out of use for a long time. Thinking of how to pull the dead body out of the well, the constable, the village Patil and Fauzdar discussed something and the constable ordered Damu finally to pull the body out. But the Fauzdar cracked his whip at Damu. The attitude the constable and the Fauzdar showed towards Damu resulted in self-realisation. Unable to tolerate the discrimination, Damu stood up and gripped the half-raised whip. As the constables always prove the power of their sticks on Dalits, the two policemen severely punished Damu until he lost senses. Jadav writes, "He (Damu) lost all sense of what was happening as he lay on the ground, jerking and convulsing at every blow and whiplash as it landed on his body."(9) Damu who was bold enough to face the punishment to any extent cried out with all his might. Patil rushed forward and pleaded with the Fauzdar to forgive Damu.

At home, all the family members found fault with Damu and said that he committed a grave mistake by disobeying the order of the Fauzdar. They scolded Damu that he had broken the Mahar's tradition by challenging the government officials. Listening to his family members, Damu said "What kind of a tradition is this that treats Mahar's worse than cats and dogs? (10) Damu was ready to face death but strongly decided not to go to yeskar duties. The incident suggests how Damu was able to face the Fauzdar. He believed in dignity, which he had learnt from Dr Ambedkar and his philosophy.

III

Omprakash Valmiki writes in *Joothan: A Dalit's Life* (2003) that the upper and other caste people live in one side of the village pond. The Chuhras and the low caste untouchables live on the other side. The pond stood as partition between the Chuhras and the rest of the village dwellers. Chuhras did all sorts of work for the upper castes, including cleaning and agricultural work. They would often work without pay. Valmiki writes:

> Nobody dared to refuse this unpaid work for which we got neither money nor grain. Instead we got sworn at and abused. They did not call us by our names. If a person were older, then he would be called 'Oe Chuhre'. If the person was younger or of the same age, then 'Abey Chuhre' was used. (Valmiki, 2)[7]

The Dalits were not properly paid for their labour. The Chuhras were not considered human. Omprakash Valmiki writes about the experience of humiliation and social discrimination in school. Hiram Singh, one of Valmiki's friends, was married off. When Hiram Singh went to bride's home as a matter of custom, the bridegroom would go to greet the people at the houses where his mother-in-law worked. When Hiram Singh went with Valmiki, the upper caste women behaved insultingly. At every home, where Hiram's mother-in-law worked, the drummer stopped and Hiram's mother-in-law called out the women of the home very politely. Hiram's mother-in-law would say, "Chaudhrian, do I have three or four other daughters that any other sons–in–law will come to your door? Please give something so that I can send my daughter away honourably..." (31)

Though Hiram's mother had been working for a long time, there was no change in the treatment of the upper caste women, who would comment, "The stomachs of these Chuhras are never filled."(31) The women offered one-rupee note to Hiram Singh. The women commented, "However much you study...you will still remain a Chuhra."(32) Therefore, Valmiki argued with his father Chotalal to abandon this kind of practice. In response, his father said, "Munshiji, [Valmiki's nickname] sending you to school has been a success... I, too, have understood your point...We will now break this custom". (32) Valmiki's father refused to send his sons to Salaam. Valmiki's education brought a tremendous change in his family.

Another incident of discrimination that Valmiki reveals is his experience at Tyagi Inter College in Muzaffarnagar. In the Tyagi Inter College, Phool Singh Tyagi was the physical education teacher. Phool Singh Tyagi punished the children for silly reasons. Once Ram Singh, a Chuhra by caste, was severely punished by Phool Singh. For that simple reason Phool Singh Tyagi commented Ram Singh, "Abey brother-in-law, progeny of a Chuhra, let me know when you die. You think you are a hero. Today I am going to draw oil from tresses."(47) Though all the other teachers and the Principal were watching the scene, no one stopped Phool Singh because they could not worry about the Chuhra boy. Valmiki writes:

> Whatever effect the beating had on Surjan Singh, this is humane act remains fresh in my memory. The same terror overtakes my consciousness when I think of that day Surjan Singh had not done anything and yet he was beaten up. If laughing was a crime, we had all laughed. Then why was only Surjan Singh punished. (48)

The incident lead to Surjan Singh's indifference to his studies and went back to Dehradun. The upper caste

Tyagis always tried to humiliate Valmiki by calling his caste 'Chuhra.'

Another incident is about Valmiki's experience at Brajpal Singh Tyagi's place. He was a Chemistry teacher at Tyagi Inter College. One day Brijpal Singh Tyagi asked Bhikuram to go to his village near Devband. Valmiki felt excited to accompany Bhikuram and left for the village by bicycle. The two boys reached the village. They started their journey early in the morning and reached the teacher's village. After that the boys were called in to have lunch. When food was ready to be served, Valmiki was hesitant due to his low caste status. After having the meal, Bhikuram sat down and Valmiki was standing at a short distance from the elder one. The elder one, knowing the two boys from Barla, asked Straight way, "What is your caste?"

Valmiki answered, "We are of the Chuhra caste." (51)

Listening to Valmiki's caste, the old man lifted a heavy stick and hit Bhikhuram on his back. Supporting the old man, many people suggested that the two boys should be tied to a rope and hung from the trees. This incident disturbed Valmiki.

The Tyagi teachers too had insulted the untouchable children for very baseless reasons. Valmiki wrote about the cruel behaviour of Omdatta Tyagi, an upper caste English teacher. Whenever Valmiki approached Omdatta either on academic or personal problems, he made Valmiki aware of his caste, Bangi. In 1965, when Valmiki was in class eleven, Narendra Kumar Tyagi was appointed as a lecturer of mathematics. Once, Narendra Kumar Tyagi asked Valmiki to go and bring him a glass of water from the pitcher. Valmiki said to him, "Master Saheb, I am not permitted even to touch those pitchers. Please send someone else." As the master asked for the reason, Valmiki replied quietly "I belong to the Chuhra caste." and continued, "If you still want me to get you water, I will go."(64-65) The master said, "No, sit down." and went himself to get water. Valmiki opines that the teacher was a coward and did not have courage to drink water from his hand.

Valmiki joined DAV College, Dehradun. He lived in Indresh Nagar, a distant village from Dehradun. But he never missed the first class which starts at 7 a.m. Valmiki and his friend came to know about the Ordnance Factory, Dehradun and abandoned his college education. Valmiki writes, "I knew absolutely nothing about the work before my induction into the factory. All I knew was that I don't want to go into the line of work that my ancestor had been doing for thousands of years."(77) Valmiki left for Jabalpur and later to Bombay for draftsman training. Wherever he went, humiliation and discrimination accompanied him. In Bombay, Valmiki got met Sadahiv Kulkari, a Maharashtrian Brahmin, whose family did not know that Valmiki was a Chuhra. Once, Valmiki met Professor Kamble at the Kulkarni's place. Mrs Kulkarni offered the Prof Kamble a cup of tea. While drinking tea, Valmiki noticed Kamble's cup which was different from the cups offered to the rest of them. Latter Valmiki came to know about it, "As I listened to him, my ears started to boil as though someone had poured mercury into them."(95)

Valmiki's interaction with Kulkarni's family led to Kulkarni's daughter, Savitha falling in love with him. She thought that Valmiki was a Brahmin. When she had learnt the caste of Valmiki, she started to cry. Valmiki writes, "She started cry as though my being an SC was a crime. She sobbed for a log time. Suddenly the distance between us had increased. The hatred of thousands of years had entered our hearts. What a lie culture and civilisation are."(98). The caste led to the permanent separation between Savitha and Valmiki and they never met again.

After getting job in the Ordnance Factory in Chanda [Chandrapur], Valmiki married Chandakala whom he calls Chanda. In Chandrapur Valmiki got acquainted with many people and he met Kureishi at Poetry reading. Kureishi was a Sub-Inspector of Police. Valmiki and Kureishi became good friends and whenever Kureishi went on night duty, he left his wife at Valmiki's place. Once Valmiki was informed by Kureishi that the new Commandant of the DSC has come on transfer from Valmiki's place. Though Valmiki had secondary interest in meeting the new DSC, Kureishi convinced him to go and meet the DSC. Valmiki and Kureishi left for the DSC's bungalow. As soon as Kureishi introduced Valmiki to the DSC, the DSC asked about the caste of Valmiki, "The moment I said that my caste was Chuhra, he became uneasy. Suddenly all conversation stopped as though there was nothing left to talk about". (115) Though it was common experience to Valmiki, it was new for Kureishi. The next day when Kureishi met the Commandant, the latter said:

> Kureishi Saheb, he is considered a low caste in our district. He and his likes are not allowed to cross the threshold, and here you are socialising with him, even dining with him.(115)

From that moment onwards, Kureishi did not meet the Commandant as Valmiki and he grew closer.

Valmiki had been insulted everywhere because of his 'Chuhra' tag. He states, "The last part of my name which is also called the surname, has landed me in a lot of dire situations because of its function as a marker of caste."(127). Some of Valmiki's friends considered his surname a signifier of a courageous act, "when an untouchable, a person from a caste considered low, uses his caste name as his surname, with a feeling of self-assertion, he is being very brave." But one gentleman commented, "What is so brave about that? ... After all, his is a Chuhra. His surname spares us the hassle of asking what his caste is." (124)

The family members of Valmiki also were bothered by his surname. Valmiki's wife Chanda preferred their gotra name 'Khairwal' instead of Valmiki. Despite being illiterate, Valmiki's father had been pleased when he found out that Valmiki used his last name. But Valmiki's wife had different mindset about using his surname 'Valmiki'. She said to Valmiki, "If we had a child, I would definitely have made you change your surname."(126) Whenever Valmiki heard such comments from his wife, he reacted "Yet such comments do torment me. I become unsettled when I hear them."(126)

Valmiki experienced discrimination within the family due to his surname. He found his name missing in the list of names on the wedding card of Manju, one of his relatives, "It is easy to battle against the outsiders; the most arduous battle has to be fought against one's own." (129) Yet, he did not give up his determination and stood as a symbol of self assertion. Getting inspiration from Valmiki, Mahendra Bainiwal, an emerging poet expressed his desire to use 'Valmiki' as his surname. Valmiki writes, "We Valmiki and Bainiwal had a long correspondence on the matter. He used Valmiki for some time but later changed to Bainiwal." (130)

Once Valmiki was invited to give a lecture on 'Buddhist Literature and Philosophy' at a conference. A member of the audience shouted, "How can a 'Valmiki' be allowed to speak on Buddhist literature and philosophy? Aren't you ashamed?" (131). But Valmiki silenced him with his excellent speech on the pervasive spread of casteism in the Hindu society.

In 1980, Valmiki was returning to Chandrapur from a trip to Rajasthan. Valmiki and his wife have seats in the Pink City express from Jaipur. Near them, there was a prosperous family, husband, wife, and two small children. They entered into a conversation. The officer's wife asked, "what is your caste?"(133) and before his wife replied, Valmiki answered that they belonged to 'Bangi.' Since then, there was no communication between the two families during the rest of the journey. Valmiki writes, "A wall had come up between us, as though we had disturbed their enjoyment by encroaching on them through a trap door. The atmosphere had turned oppressive, the journey had become very painful. (133)

To overcome the experiences of discrimination, Valmiki develop resilience. Valmiki writes:

> When caste is the basis of respect and merit, important for social superiority, this battle can't be won in a day. We need an ongoing struggle, and a consciousness of struggle a consciousness that brings revolutionary change both in the outside world and in the our hearts a consciousness that leads the process of social change." (132)

Similar to the experiences of discrimination by Limbale and Jadav, Valmiki also traces out the genesis of the caste discrimination and its influence on Dalit even among the educated.

IV

Baby Kamble's *The Prisons We Broke* (2008) is considered the manifesto of Dalit women. Maya Pandit observes, "Like most Dalit autobiographies, *The Prisons We Broke* is an expression of protest against the inhuman conditions of existence to which the Hindu caste system has subjected the Dalit for thousands of years?"[8] She notes that after Phule and Shahu Maharaj, it was

Dr Babasaheb Ambedkar who provided the intellectual and ideological foundations for a sustained critique of the caste system and that under the leadership of Dr Ambedkar, Dalit protest acquired the form and force of a militant political movement and challenged the very foundations of Hinduism.

Baby Kamble raises certain important issues like caste discrimination, women subjugation and the influence of Dr Ambedkar on Dalit women to get themselves educated both socially and culturally. Kamble writes about caste discrimination that the poor Mahars went under. Mahars were treated as untouchable servants 'yeskars.' By doing yeskar jobs, the Mahars would get bhakris (leftover food) which they eat after drying them in the sun. Mahars are not allowed to use the regular road that is used by the upper castes. Kamble writes, "When somebody from these castes walked from the opposite direction, the Mahars had to leave the road, climb down into the shrubbery and walk through the thorny bushes on the road side."(Kamble, 52)[9]

The Mahar women would beg for the mercy of the upper castes. Every new bride had to adopt and follow this custom. If they failed, they would be severely warned by the upper castes as well as Mahars. If anyone failed to beg for mercy of the upper castes, the master would simply explode in rage and come straight to the Mahar chawdi and call the new bride a shameless bitch. Kamble writes, "Who, just tell me, who the hell is that new girl? Doesn't she know that she has to bow down to the master? Shameless bitch! How dare she pass me without showing due respect?" (53)

The elderly women from the Mahar community would fall on the feet of the master and beg for his mercy. The poor Mahars would request the master, "No, no kind master! The girl is a new animal in the herd! Quite foolish and ignorant. If she has erred, I, her sasra, fall at your feet, but please forgive us for this crime." (53) The newly married bride is called 'an animal in the herd' and whatever she did is treated as crime.

From the foregoing discussion, it may be understood that the institutionalisation of caste and untouchability in the Hindu social order cause insult and humiliation to the Dalits leading to forced exclusion and isolation. The Dalits are physically excluded from the high caste locality in rural area. The Dalits are not entitled to any civic, social, cultural and religious rights. The social movements and education resulted in the growth of self-respect and assertion of the Dalit self. The four autobiographies that have been examined are indicative of the fact that solution to the discrimination lies in the self-respect and asserting the self. Sharan Kumar Limbale, Narendra Jadav, Omprakash Valmiki and Baby Kamble proved in their respective autobiographies that the Dalits need not be ashamed of their caste. Liberation from the Dalit discrimination and humiliation lies in self-respect.

The following chapter "Writing Dalit Gender: Dalit among Dalits" focuses on the aspect of the aspects of Dalit gender.

References

1. Limbale, Sharan Kumar, *The Outcaste*, New Delhi, OUP, 2003, 36. (Subsequent references to this addition with page numbers are given in parenthesis).
2. Impure, incomplete, an illegitimate child.
3. Kolakaluri Enoch, *Oorabaavi* (Public Well), 1969.
4. Purushotham, K., *Evolution of Telugu Dalit Literature*, *Economic and Political Weekly*, Vol. XLV, No. 22, May 29, 2010.

5. Jadav, Narendra, *Outcaste*: New Delhi, Oxford University Press, 2003, IX. (Subsequent references to this addition with page numbers are given in parenthesis).

6. A village servant.

7. Valmiki, Omprakash, *Joothan: A Dalit's Life*, New Delhi: Sage, 2003, 2. (Subsequent references to this addition with page numbers are given in parenthesis).

8. Kamble, Baby, *The Prisons We Broke*, New Delhi: Orient Longman, 2008, vii.

9. Kamble, Baby, 52. (Subsequent references to this addition with page numbers are given in parenthesis).

4

Writing Dalit Gender: Dalit Among Dalits

This chapter sets out to explore the significance of Dalit gender and its construction by examining Baby Kamble's *The Prisons We Broke* (2008). An attempt is made in this chapter to study the evolution of Dalit gender as a separate entity that demands its own autonomy in terms of literature, culture and political domains. Baby Kamble, who has been influenced by Ambedkar movement and its ideology, sets an agenda that Ambedkar's ideology is the right solution for the emancipation of women in the Indian context. She exhorts that Ambedkar has envisaged an egalitarian society by introducing Hindu Code Bill in the Parliament for the upliftment of the Indian women.

I

This section examines the evolution of the Dalit feminism. The terms 'sex', 'gender' and 'feminism' need to be qualified to understand them in the present context. Sex refers to the biological aspect; gender indicates the culture of sociological and political dominance of men over women; feminism, as a theory questions the gender dominance based on sex. The subordination of women had been fundamentally justified on the grounds of the biological differences between men and women. The subordination of women needs to be theorised for it helps in challenging, subverting and expending not only other (male) theories but its own positions and agenda.[1]

Both feminism and post-colonialism share the mutual goal of challenging forms of oppression. The Western feminist criticism argued against the three fold dominance. According to Peter Barry, "Debates and disagreements have centred on three particular areas, these being: the role of theory; the nature of language, and the value or otherwise of psychoanalysis."[2] The Western feminist theory questioned the dominance of gender. Indian feminist critics like Kamla Bhasin and Nishat Said Khan opine that feminism is based on historically and culturally concentrate realities and levels of consciousness, perceptions and actions.[3]

Madhu Kishwar draws a line between Western feminism and feminism in India, "In the West, feminism undoubtedly played a liberating role for women, feminism evolved from women's own struggles against oppressive power structures which excluded them from equal participation in many aspects of the economic, social and political life of their society."[4] In India, new opportunities were made available for a small number of Western educated women who gravitated towards feminism. Indian feminism is Western imported and failed in studying the sociological problems that come across sex and gender dominance. Indian feminism failed in studying women in the light of caste and it could be called exclusivist feminism. Madhu Kishwar observes that both Western and Indian feminists fought for their entry into educational institutions, employment and power structures. In this context, it is important to note that Dalit and tribal women are excluded from voting, education and employment.

Kancha Ilaiah argues that for a long time the position of women was perceived as a private domain, and therefore political scientists took little interest in studying the views of both male and female thinkers on women. Greek thinkers like Plato and Aristotle have developed a narrow kind of opinion on women. Ilaiah writes, "on the one hand, Plato provided provision for equal education and equal right to become philosopher queens to women belonging to the upper class and on the other he believed that the female sex was created from the souls of the most wicked and irrational men.[5] Women are granted equal rights to education but attainable only by the ruling class. Aristotle seems to represent more reactionary patriarchal thinking, "Women are naturally inferior to men, and that they are therefore naturally ruled by them...Women's main function is reproduction. The man via his semen always provides the soul of the offspring, while the female via her menstrual discharge provides the matter."[6] Regarding Manu's views on women, Ilaiah elaborates:

> Manu deprived women of their basic political rights even at home. Forbidden to decide anything for herself, she was to be completely deprived of her initiative...If a woman flouted this law, according to him, society should condemn her, and the sovereign should punish her.[7]

Ilaiah criticises Kautilya's views on women that Kautilya had the intentional view that every married woman was to be kept strictly under control and constant surveillance: .

> According to him, every married woman was to be kept strictly under control and constant surveillance

> trade relations into the marriage system. He gave enormous powers to the state to punish and fine them if they did not behave according to Arthashastra law...Thus, Kautilya did not consider the home a private place, but one where the state could intervene for every small violation of patriarchal- brahminical law, even within the four walls. Like Manu's law, Kautilya also did not grant social and political rights to married women.[8]

Regarding Vatsayana's arguments, Ilaiah states that Vatsayana categorised Hindu women into two types. They were the *ganikas* and the wives. The *ganikas* are meant for giving sexual pleasure to men and the wives are with the duty of producing the off-spring:

> Vatsayana reduced the position of women to mere toys in the hands of men by prescribing at length what a *ganika* should do to keep a customer happy. He gave a detailed list of things that a citizen should possess: the decorated rooms and equipment for feasts and festivals where the women could be used for amusement.[9]

Vatsayana had not visualised any place for women in politics and state affairs. Manu gave the men right to punish women, Kautilya gave powers to the state to punish and penalise women. Vatsayana reduced the position of women to mere objects in the hands of men at sex. The Hindu thinkers, argues Ilaiah, provided a theoretical framework for the enslavement of women within the framework of the monogamous family. Chastity, prostitution, marriage and every institutional arrangement was used to reduce the position of a woman to that of a slave.

The Western and the Hindu thinkers provided a theoretical framework for the enslavement of women within the framework of the monogamous family. In contrast, the philosophy of Lord Buddha strengthened women to encounter the limitations and personal ambivalences. Ilaiah enlists five significant points of Buddhism about women:

> With all his limitations and personal ambivalences about women, Buddha can be credited with five significant achievements: (i) Buddha recognised the political right of women to join the sangha; (ii) he forced the sangha to recognise women's right to be leaders; (iii) against the dominant Hindu view, Buddha held that a women can develop her own personality and individuality independent of any male support; (iv) he broke the myth of family and the importance of producing male children to attain salvation; and (v) he was the first to recognise the need for women's education and political initiative.[10]

Another significant move in favour of women is the arrival of Bhakti Saint Poets who challenged the Brahmanical hegemony in India. A Dalit critic G. Aloysius calls the 'Bhakti' school of saint poets the 'Mukti' Poets. Aloysius has the sense that all the Mukti Saint poets have strived for the devotional liberation. The Bhakti poets represent a cultural revolt. The Bhakti poets are from different backgrounds but the common goal they had is to debrahmanise India.

The Bhakti poets Basava, Haralayya, Akka Mahadevi from Karataka, Namdev, Chokhamela, Tukaram and Savata Mali from Maharashtra, Kabir, Ravidas, Dadu Dayal, Rajput princess Mira, Kranti Nanak, the potter Gora and the barber Sena from North region of India Pothuluri Veerabrahman, Yogivemana and Nagadass from Thumulur in Andhra questioned the dominant historiography of Hindu religion and its orthodoxy.

Braj Ranjan Mani states, "The general backdrop of the [Bhakti] movement was the chaos in the wake of the Muslim invasions, the worsening economic conditions, and poverty made worse by the Brahmanical lightening of socio-religious restrictions."[11] The Bhakti poets' emphasis lies on spiritual equality, social justice and deep sympathy for the common people. According to Braj Rajan Mani:

> Many Bhakti leaders, particularly Kabir and Nanak, transcended sectarian differences and consciously incorporated the bright elements of all faiths, including Islam, in their teachings. They protested against the low position given to women and encouraged them to join their men folk in various activities. When the followers of Kabir, Ravidas and Nanak gathered together women were included in the gathering.[12]

Following Buddhism and Christianity, the Bhakti movement gave vital importance for the development of women. Apart from the depressed women, the non-Brahman women also took active part in the Bhakti movement. For example, Mirabai, the Rajasthan Rajput princess who was known for her finest hymns in Hindi become a disciple of Ravidas, an untouchable saint. Braj Ranjan Mani states that a high caste princess taking a guru from among the untouchables represents a rebellion against the casteism and patriarchy of the medieval society.[13]

Virashaiva movement in Karnataka, one of the counterparts of Bhakti movement is known for the combination of egalitarianism and spiritual excellence. Braj Ranjan Mani writes:

> A sparkling feature of Virashaivism is the strong presence of women who played a significant role in

> the movement. There were many influential female ascetics in early Virashaivism...The movement severely criticised the brahminical legitimation of female subordination and tried to build a new version on the man-woman relationship. It was characteristic of Vishaivism that there was place in it for the most unconventional of women like Akka Mahadevi and Muktayakka.[14]

The philosophy of Hinduism and Brahmin domination lowered the women's status. But it is only through the Bhakti Movements, the women of suppressed castes and anti-Brahmin women like the princess of Rajput Mirabai, Akkamahadevi and Muktayakka take active part, accepting the untouchable saints as their gurus.

Uma Chakravarti points out that there are many references to caste and gender discrimination in the *abhagas,* the poems written by Bhakti saints. This kind of secondary citizenship in terms of gender paved the way for the emergence of Bhakti School of women saints. Uma Chakravarti locates a number of women saints that include Muktabai, Bahinabai, Soyarabai, Kannopatra and Janabai, among others, who questioned the gender discrimination.[15]

The philosophy of Lord Buddha and the movements led by Bhakti Saints influenced Mahatma Jotibha Phule and Babasaheb Ambedkar, the architects of modern India. Mahatma Jotibha Phule (1827–1890) was the first activist to launch a movement in India for the liberation of the Sudras, Dalits and women. Phule is the ideological and political founder of the anti-caste movement. He saw a close relationship between knowledge and power much before Foucault and Edward Said.[16] Phule adopted a more radical approach to gender inequality than any of his contemporaries.[17]

Phule understood that exclusion from knowledge was the main cause behind women's subordination and education was the key aspect to liberate them. Phule and his wife Savitribai established 18 schools between 1848 and 1852. They established a separate school for girls in India in 1948 and it was the first school meant for depressed girl children. In 1860s, Phule actively campaigned for widow remarriage and fought for banning the practice of child marriage. Phule, sensitive to gender, was conscious of the differences within women based on caste and productive culture. In his view the low caste women are doubly oppressed as they are oppressed both by the upper caste men and the men of their own families.

B.R. Ambedkar constructed his theory based on the teachings of Buddha, Kabir and Phule. He identified caste and patriarchy as the twin forces that arrest the progression of Dalit women. To root out gender inequality, Ambedkar introduced the Hindu Code Bill in 1951, which envisaged the social security of women in India. It was, however, not allowed to be passed by the upper caste leadership who wanted the orthodox Hindu practices to be continued.[18] Challapalli Swaroopa Rani writes that the contribution of Ambedkar in educating Dalit women is unforgettable. She also states Ambedkar dealt with the human relations on one hand and highlighted the need for co-ordination between male and female: "In India, both women and Dalits are equally exploited and strategically excluded because of caste. Ambedkar did a war against these two social evils."[19]

Contemporary feminist critics Meenakshi Moon and Urmila Pawar write, "women actively involved in the early Untouchable Liberation Movement" and liberated many women out of the *Devadasi* profession and find husbands for them as early as 1908.[20] In the movements like Mahad Satyagraha of 1928, Nasik Satyagraha to enter the Kalaram temple (1930–35) in which Ambedkar declared that he 'would not die a Hindu,' hundreds of women held independent conference to support Dr Ambedkar's declaration to convert.[21]

Eleanor Zelliot examined the involvement of women in Ambedkar movement and other women organisations. She writes:

> Vimal Throat reports that the National Federation of Dalit Women, as a code to the Mahad Conference of 1927, which are seen as the real beginning of the Ambedkar movement, has called for Dalits to gather at Mahad again on December 25, 1998. Just as the Mahad Conference of December 25, 1927, burned those portions of the Manusmriti which limited the rights of Untouchables and legalised extreme punishments for any supposed transgression, the Mahad Conference of December 25, 1998 will find women in the thousands burning the *Manusmriti* for its denial of human rights to women.[22]

Highly influenced by Ambedkar Movement, many Dalit writers in the post-Ambedkar period produced excellent works, who include, Urmila Pawar, Jyoti Langewar, Hira Bansode, Surekha Bhagat, Pradnya Lokhande, Mina Gajbhiye, Baby Kamble, Shantabai Kamble among others. Telugu has produced such stalwarts as Challapalli Swaroopa Rani, Gogu Syamala, Vinodini and Jupaka Subadra and Siva Kami, Bama and Veeramma have been writing powerful works in Tamil. Writing about the emergency of Dalit Feminist literature and its need, Challapalli Swaroopa Rani states:

> It has a long time for Dalit women to overcome their oppression, as Dalits and put to creative use the gains of social and literary movements. There are of course

> common issues that bind Dalit men and women, like untouchability and caste oppression. But women also suffer from patriarchal oppression. These concerns are constantly foregrounded in Dalit women's poetry in Telugu and are evident in the form, content and the emotions that they express. However, Dalit women's poetry in Telugu still needs to develop beyond the confines of patriarchy.[23]

She further states that the poetry by Dalit women is far more powerful and has a far greater impact than the poetry of Dalit male poets or upper caste women poets. Dalit women's issues have less in common with Dalit men's issues when compared to those of the upper caste women.

In the post-Ambedkar period, Dalit women used literature as a weapon to counter the mainstream feminist writing that include the genres, like poetry, short story, essay, novel and autobiography. Of all the genres, the autobiography is found suitable to write the women's experiences in their local idiom. The Dalit women's autobiographies include, Bama's *Karruku* (2004), Viramma Josiane Racine's *Viramma: Life of a Dalit* (1997) in Tamil and Urmila Pawar's *The Weave of Life* (2009) and Baby Kamble's *The Prisons We Broke* (2008) in Marathi. Jasbir Jain writes that ordinarily the autobiographical form presents a consciousness of the 'self' which retrospectively traces the process of the self-evolution. The autobiographical narratives work backwards in time, and are selective in the choice of events which have impacted the writer. Further she identifies that the gender is an important category for women's autobiography.[24] The following section examines Baby Kamble's *The Prisons We Broke* as a text representing the aspect of the double oppression of the Dalit women.

II

Baby Kamble presents in *The Prisons We Broke* (2008) the development of herself as well as her community. In an interview with her translator Maya Pandit, she says, "I wrote about what my community experienced. The suffering of my people became my own suffering. Their experiences become mine. So I really find it very difficult to think of myself outside of my community." (Kamble, 136)[25]

The narration deals with her family background, village customs like worshipping local deities, superstitions, Mahars and yeskar duties, school education, experiences of discrimination, marriage customs, experiences of new brides with their in-laws, cooking beef, Dalit culture, exploitation of the upper castes, the influence of movies, the influence of Buddha and finally the arrival of Dr Ambedkar as Dalit messiah and Kamble's active involvement in Ambedkar movement.

The experience of insecurity is one among the major aspects in Kamble's autobiography. The position of Dalit women in a Dalit family, which is full of experiences charred by insecurity, domestic violence and social violence, is an important theme in her autobiography. The patriarchal system in India made the Dalit women feel insecure and dependant on men.

Stating the importance of sons in a family, Baby Kamble writes, "The eldest son was the pride of the house. He would be offered to the deity as *vaghya* or *potraja*. Fathers had a loin's share in preparing their sons for this role. To offer the son as *vaghya* or *potraja* was considered a great honour and prestige for the family. The father very diligently saw to it that his son was properly trained." (18-19) The elder sons are given high priority and the prestige of daughters is not considered by the parents.

Another aspect of domestic violence that Dalit women experience is the hegemony of husband and the dominance of in-laws at the bridegroom's place. The author illustrates, "But we too were human beings. And we too desired to dominate, to wield power. But who would let us do that? So we made our own arrangements to find slaves – our very own daughters-in-law! If nobody else then we could at least enslave them." (87) She writes that young girls, hardly eight or nine or ten years old, were brought home as daughters-in-law. Girls, even younger were married off. There were children who could not even remember their marriages.

Baby Kamble presents how marriages take place among Dalit families even when the bride or bridegrooms are very young. Raja Ram Mohan Roy, however dealt with the child marriages in Hindu families. Being a young bride, a Hindu woman experiences patriarchy at domestic level. But a Dalit woman experiences violence at home and caste discrimination in public places. In this context, Dalit women experience double alienation. Kamble describes:

> Thus, girl would embark upon a new life that was harsh and arduous. She was a young girl, a child really, still immature. Yet, the poor child had to break all ties of love and go to her in-laws' house to lead a married life, without even knowing what a husband meant, or what it was to be given away. (93)

As soon as the bride arrives at her in-laws' home, she would be asked to make two baskets full bhakris. The new bride is not allowed to sleep until she completes the entire household duties. Baby Kamble also deals with how Dalit women are confined to live within the four walls of the house, "In those days, it was the custom to keep women at home, behind the threshold. The honour enjoyed by a family was in proportion to the restrictions imposed on the women of the house."(5)

The author depicts the experiences of social discrimination by the Dalit women. She writes that a Dalit woman needs to stand in the courtyard keeping a distance from the shopkeeper. She would beg him with utmost humility to sell her the things she wanted, "Appasab, could you please give this despicable Mahar woman some shikaki for one paisa and half a shell of dry coconut with black skin."(13) If the shopkeeper's children trickle out into the courtyard for their morning ablutions, the shopkeeper would give the innocent children lessons in social behaviour:

> 'Chabu, hey you can't you see the dirty Mahar woman standing there? Now don't you touch her? Keep your distance'. Immediately our Mahar women, gathering her rags around her tightly so as not to pollute the child, would say, 'Take care little master! Please keep a distance. Don't come too close. You might touch me and get polluted.' The shopkeeper would come out and, from a distance, throw the things into her pallav, which she had spread out in order to receive them. She would then respectfully keep her money on the threshold. That of course did not pollute him. (13-14)

The Dalit women undergo severe caste discrimination and violence. Baby Kamble recounts how the Dalit women are not allowed to use the regular road that was used by the higher castes writes:

> When somebody from these castes walked from the opposite direction, the Mahars had to leave the road, climb down into the shrubbery and walk through the thorny bushes on the roadside. They had to cover

> themselves fully if they saw any man from the higher castes close, they had to say, 'The humble Mahar woman fall at your feet master'. This was like a chant, which they had to repeat innumerable times, even to a small child if it belonged to higher caste. (52)

Mahar women find it difficult to face the discrimination at the work places. The Brahmin women consider that their mere touch pollutes them while buying firewood from them: "The Mahar women would check the bundles carefully, saying, 'Kaki, we have taken out every stand of hair and thread from the sticks. Each stick has been checked. Have we gone mad that we will pollute your house? You are god's own people. Don't we know even that?"(55) The Brahmin women do not allow their children to play if the Mahar women are on the business of selling firewood.

Kamble narrates how the Dalit women are made to suffer because of the orthodox belief of the Hinduism, "The entire community had sunk deep in the mire of such dreadful superstitions. The upper castes had never allowed this lowly caste of ours to acquire knowledge. Generations after generations, our people rotted and perished by following such a superstitions way of life. Yet, we kept believing in your Hindu religion and serving you faithfully."(37) She writes that the fear of death drove people to goddess Satwai and they would perform all the customary rituals. The Brahmin priests intimidate the Dalit women so that they do not question them.

Baby Kamble narrates an accident that reflects the extent of superstitions in the lives of the Dalit women: "We must now give up eating dead animals. Ambedkar knows what he is saying. He has been educated in the white man's land. Is he mad to say so without a reason? He says this because he knows something about it. It is time to discard this maharness...Don't eat dead animals."(66) But Karbhari who was a man of old customs and traditions did not accept Bhaikai Anji's suggestion and said: "How dare you ask us to give up our custom of eating dead animals! You are asking us to revolt against the village...the village land is our mother. We have to carry forward whatever order she has given us. Why do we need foreign Knowledge?"(66-67) Karbhari termed Ambedkar's knowledge as foreign and labeled that yeskar's stick was the mark of the happiness of the land and they had in them real Mahar flesh and blood.

This incident between Aaja and Karbhari represents the struggle between Ambedkar's knowledge which is termed foreign and the ignorance of the Mahars. They also said that the yeskar's staff was not just an ordinary stick with a bell. It was no less than a royal staff; it was the mark of the real strength of the Mahar who was a proud breed.

Even the poor, illiterate and ignorant Mahar's did not find fault to offer young girls to the village goddess Ambabai as jogins and young boys as potrajas. As they have been practicing this custom of offering young boys and girls to the goddess for ages, they never dare to come out of it. They blindly believe that the Goddess Ambabai will give blessings and the remaining Mahars will be protected. The poor Mahars say, "We have been doing so for ages; that's why we have his blessings and our children are protected. And the jogin? She is also a women offered to our goddess. And you don't want to do any of this? Do you know that if the goddess is displeased, she can ruin the entire house? She will burn our houses as punishment. The potraja is supposed to be the servant of the goddess."(67-68)

Baby Kamble states that people used to be afflicted with typhoid in the Maharwada. If anybody suffered from malaria, they believed that one was possessed by Hadal, a female ghost. Epidemics like cholera and plague used to be common among the Mahars, and they depend on superstitions:

> When the patient had fits, ten strong men would sit on his chest and a couple of others pin his legs down. The onlookers would watch the scene in horrified fascination. They would wonder aloud about the terrible strength of the spirit possessing the man. 'What a powerful spirit!' they would exclaim. 'Ten men cannot control him! We have seen it with our own eyes'. (80-81)

Internalisation of the patriarchy is another aspect that Baby Kamble deals with. A Dalit woman who experienced the patriarchy and caste shows authority over her daughter-in-law. Baby Kamble writes:

> In those days, at least one woman in a hundred would have her nose chopped off. You may well ask why. It's because of the *sasu*, who would poison her son's mind. These *sasus* ruined the lives of innocent women forever...They had no food to eat, no proper clothing to cover their bodies; their hair would remain uncombed and tangled, dry from lack of oil. Women led the most miserable existence.(98)

Kamble further depicts how the young girls are beaten up:

> Once she was brought back to her in-laws, an even worse fate awaiting her. Her in-laws would take a huge square piece of wood – weighing around five kilos – to the carpenter to have stocks made for her. The carpenter would drill a hole in the wood, big enough for her foot to go through. After this, they would put an iron bar through the sides so as to make it impossible for her to pull an iron tub. She would

> have to drag this heavy burden each time she tired to move...She was not a human being for her in-laws, but just another piece of wood. (98-99)

In Dalit families, Dalit women work equally as their men do. They work at home as well as in the fields. She further states that Dr Ambedkar's made the Mahar women to take a different path. Ambedkar asked the Mahar women to educate their children so that they will make the Mahar women aware of their rights. Influenced by Ambedkar's speech, Bhaikai Anji made a resounding speech:

> Let me assure you, my sisters, what right. We must educate our children. We must not and will not eat dead animals. We must reform our community. Let us resolve to fight along with Ambedkar. He speaks nothing but the truth. Let's follow him to the end. This is what I say. (65)

Ambedkar's speech caught the attention of the Dalit women, and Baby Kamble was one among them: "I am a product of the Ambedkar movement...Ambedkar taught us that character is the foundation of this edifice called the human society. When compassion and morality follow character, society achieves its real strength. He wanted to transform society in the light of this philosophy."(125)

The author recollects the cunning nature of the upper castes. Hinduism confined the women to the superstitions and rituals:

> Today many of our daughters and daughters-in-law are graduates. They are a hundred times more superior to ignorant women like us. Even if their husbands forget the father in the glory of their own so called greatness, it is their duty to reprimand their husbands. They should tell them, 'Remember, what you are today is solely because of Dr Babasaheb Ambedkar.(123)

To overcome this handicap, the Mahar women began to think rationally. Influenced by Ambedkar, Baby Kamble as a school going girl dared to pollute Rama in protest against not being allowed into the Hindu temple. She considers that giving up the Hindu worship is her first active movement. Later Baby Kamble involved herself in many other activities that include the demanding for Dalit women rights. She recollects an incident. Rani Lakshmibai established the first women's club, Mahila Mandal, in Phalton, which was occupied by Brahmin women. As the Rani decided to allow Mahar women into the Mandal, the revolutionary Dalit women activists like Thakubai Kakade, Mathubai More, Fattabai Kakade and Vithabai Kakade used to take women from all the houses to the meetings held by the Mandal. Baby Kamble involved herself actively in the meetings. Kamble writes:

> All the Brahmin and Marata women had occupied the chairs. They wouldn't allow the Mahar women to sit on the chairs. Helpless, our women stood on the side. At the same time, the Ram Sahib started to move towards the stage, accompanied by her other followers Godbole, Velankar and Bhadkamkar. Our Thakubai rushed forward. (133)

The encounter of the Dalit women with Rani suggests that the Dalit women are socially educated and politically determined. The Dalit women are more radical in questioning the caste discrimination and dominance Baby Kamble also states, "Attending meetings was a new activity for our women. By now they had become more aware because of Babasaheb Ambedkar with such meetings their knowledge began to increase. They began to take firm steps ahead."(133)

She is aware of social challenges that the Dalit women face. Baby Kamble became a political activist too.

In Phalton, at the time of elections, Baby Kamble and her husband canvassed for their party candidates and participated in the demonstrations. She states that they are never out of Ambedkar's movement and she devoted herself totally to the movement. Highly inspired by Ambedkar's thoughts, she sent her children to school. She was very much inspired by Dr Ambedkar's speech:

> Educate your children. They, in turn, should spend one per cent of their salary in improving the lot of poor children only then will their education benefit the community and the generation next to their will be educated. Once they are educated, they can organise themselves and find out various ways of directing the struggle. And I am sure my sisters and mothers will carry out this task with an iron resolve. (135)

She decided to begin her struggle through her writings. She established an orphanage for the backward castes. She is the president of Mahatma Phule Duyan Vikas Prasarak Sanstha where two hundred children are studying in the school.

Thus, Baby Kamble's narration of various incidents vis-à-vis the Dalit women suggests that the nature of the problems faced by the Dalit women in India essentially differs from those that the upper caste women face. Since the nature of the problems differs, the solutions to the problems of the Dalit women too differ. As a staunch follower of Dr Ambedkar, Baby Kamble illustrates how education and self-assertion redeem the Dalit women from the kind of the domestic and social problems that the Dalit women confront.

The coming chapter "Construction of Dalit Identity: Assertion of the Self" deals with various non-Brahman and Dalit movements lead by Bhakti poets and later the influence of Phule and Adi movements that shaped the

Dalit movements into a literary movement. It is the major aspect of the study about the arrival of Dr Ambedkar which made great and influential changes on Dalit Panther's movement which leads to establish a separate literary canon for Dalits.

References

1. Raman Seldon, ed, *A Reader's Guide to Contemporary Literary Theory,* New Delhi: Pearson, 2007, 127.

2. Peter Barry, *Begginning Theory: An Introduction to Literary and Cultural Theory*, New Delhi, Viva, 2008, 123.

3. Maitraye Chaudhuri, ed, *Feminism in India: Issues in Contemporary Indian Feminism*, New Delhi: Kali for Women, 2004, 4.

4. Maitraye Chaudhuri (ed.), 44.

5. Kancha Ilaiah, *God as Political Philosopher: Buddha's Challenge to Brahmanism*, Kolkata: Samya, 2004, 200.

6. Kancha Ilaiah, 202.

7. Kancha Ilaiah, 182

8. Kancha Ilaiah, 183.

9. Kancha Ilaiah, 183-84.

10. Kancha Ilaiah, 184.

11. Braj Ranjan Mani, *Debrahmanising History: Dominance and Resistance in Indian Society*, New Delhi: Manohar, 2007, 136.

12. Braj Ranjan Mani, 154.

13. Braj Ranjan Mani, 154.

14. Braj Ranjan Mani, 166.

15. Uma Chakravarthi, *Gendering Caste through a Feminist Lens*, Calcutta: Stree 2006, 103.

16. Braj Ranjan Mani, *Debrahmanising History: Dominance and Resistance in Indian Society,* New Delhi: Manohar, 2007, 251.
17. Uma Chakravarthi, *Rewriting History: The Life and Times of Pandita Ramabai,* Delhi: Kali for Women, 1998, 65.
18. Branj Ranjan Mani, 405.
19. Challapalli Swaroopa Rani, "Dalit Feminist Literature and the influence of Ambedkar," in Dalit Voice, Hyderabad: Dalit Voice Publications, 2006, 16.
20. Eleanor Zelliot, "Dr. Ambedkar and the Empowerment of Women," in *Gender and Caste: Issues in Contemporary Indian Feminism,* ed, Anupama Rao, New Delhi: Women Unlimited and Kali for Women, 2006, 205.
21. Eleanor Zelliot, 205.
22. Eleanor Zelliot, 208.
23. Challapalli Swaroopa Rani, "Dalit Women's Writing in Telugu," in *Economic and Political Weekly*, April 25, 1998, 21.
24. Jasbir Jain, *Writing Women across Cultures,* Jaipur and New Delhi: Rawat, 2002, 281.
25. Kamble, Baby, *The Prisons We Broke,* New Delhi: Orient Black Swan, 2008, 136. Subsequent references are to this addition with page numbers given in parenthesis.

5

Construction of Dalit Identity: Assertion of the Self

There has been a long tradition of intellectual reconstruction of the Dalit identity in India. The eminent activists who contributed to the process include Phule, Periyar and Ambedkar, among others. Before them, the Bhakti saints made a remarkable contribution in the form of questioning the Brahmanical hegemony. They questioned the religious restrictions on worship during the 10th and 13th centuries, because of which the Bhakti movement became popular among the sudras and ati-shudras. This chapter explores, by referring to select Dalit autobiographies, the contribution of the Adi-movements, the non-Brahman movements against the Brahmin hegemony, Dr Ambedkar's attempts of the intellectual re-construction of the Dalit identity and the identity movements in the contemporary period leading to the culmination of the reconstruction of the Dalit identity.

I

This section explores the formation of the Dalit identity in the early period for a proper understanding of the evolution of the identity movement. Identity formation is a historical process. Identity formation is based on the experience of the Dalits in relation to the community. The experience about oneself and the community is a part of the existing socio-economic, political, cultural order. Identity as a concept is based on the experience of oneself in relation to others, similar beliefs and cultural expressions that cause to formulate the identity. This can as well be applied to the identity formation of the Dalits against the backdrop of various phases of the consciousness building movements.

The first phase of the identity formation of the Dalits may be said to be the Bhakti movement, which helped construct an identity in opposition to the Brahmin identity. The mystics who led the Bhakti movement include Ramanand and Raidas in the North, Chaitanya and Chandidasa in the East, Eknath, Choka Mela, Thukaram and Narsinh Mehta in the West and Ramanuja, Nimbaraka and Basava in the South. Their contribution to the anti-Brahmin thought lies in opposing caste distinctions and asserting equality before god. M.G. Ranade called the Bhakti movement being unbrahmanical.[1] However, the saint poets did not advocate detachment from normal worldly life as a prerequisite for the salvation. They advocated normal family life in society. Unlike the Brahmin priests, Bhakti poets disapproved of renunciation, asceticism and celibacy as the means of enlightenment. The significant contribution of the Bhakti poets is that the untouchables identified themselves as anti-brahmanical by which they formed a unique non-Brahmin identity.

Next to the Bhakti movement, the 'Adi' movements were significant in the formation of the Dalit identity. Gail Omvedt argues that "The mobilisation of the oppressed and exploited sections of society, the peasants, Dalit, women and low castes that Phule had spoken of as shudras and ati-shudras occurred on a large scale in the 1920s and 1930s, under varying leaderships and with varying ideologies."[2] The 'Non-Aryan' or the non-brahmin movements in Maharashtra and Tamil Nadu, the Dalit movements in Punjab and Karnataka were against the Aryan conquest and Brahman exploitation through religion and culture. These movements, being aimed at the argument of the original inhabitants, have a common tag 'Adi' which means original inhabitant. Most of the Dalit movements like 'Adi-Dharma' in Punjab, 'Adi-Hindu' in UP and Hyderabad, 'Adi-Dravida,' 'Adi-Andhra' and 'Adi-Karnataka' in South India have a common claim of the Dalits and Sudras being the original habitants of India. Gail Omvedt writes:

> It was in the 1920s, however, that Dalits began to organise strongly and independently through out many regions of India. The most important of the early Dalit movements were the Ad-Dharm movement in the Punjab (organised 1926); the movement under Ambedkar in Maharashtra, mainly based among Mahars which had its organisational beginnings in 1924; the Namashudra movement in Bengal; the Adi-Dravida movement in Tamil Nadu; the Adi-Karnataka movement; the Adi-Hindu movement mainly centred around Kanpur in UP; and the organising of the Pulayas and Cherumans in Kerala.[3]

The Namasudhra movement in 1972 was the first protest against the social authority of the higher castes. Sekhar Bandyopadhyay views:

> The Namasudhra movement in Bengal is the story of an antyaja or untouchable caste, transforming itself from an amphibious peripheral multitude into a settled agricultural community, protesting against the age-old social disabilities and economic exploitation it suffered from, entering the vortex of

institutional politics and trying to derive benefit out of it through an essentially loyalist political strategy.[4]

The Namashudras, earlier known as Chandals, lived mainly in the low lying swap areas of Eastern Bengal. The Namasudras or Chandals, who are considered untouchables, are originally a tribal community living in the Eastern Bengal even before the formation of the Brahmanical social order. The Namasudra movement protested against the oppressive domination of the high castes showing allegiance to the patronising colonial elite. This resulted in the emergence of backward class politics in Bengal. The Namasudras embraced Islam or Christianity to avoid the stigma of untouchability in the early twentieth century. Chandal Movement of 1872-73 led to the formation of the Namasudra led by Harichand Thakur of Faridpur and his son in the subsequent period, the movement believed in education and self-respect.

Next to Namasudra movement, Ad-Dharm movement, led by Mangoo Ram in Punjab, made a substantial contribution to the social and political life of Dalits in Punjab. He was influenced by the Ghadar movement, a radical organisation in California aimed at liberating India from British rule through armed insurrection. He opened a school for the lower caste children in the village, where the Ad-Dharm movement was launched in 1926. The movement, however, was split into two groups, the other influenced by Arya Samaj: "While the Arya Samaj was making frantic to bring Shudras who had converted to Islam, Christianity and Sikhism back into the Hindu fold, Mangoo Ram thought it appropriate to intervene at this juncture to espouse the Dalit cause and carve out a separate Dalit identity."[5]

The ideology and principles of the Ad-Dharm movement greatly influenced the Dalits of the Doaba region decisively contributing to the formation of the Dalit identity.

Adi-Hindu movement, under the leadership of Swami Acchutanand, in Uttar Pradesh is another significant movement that contributed to the construction of the Dalit identity in the 1920s. Though Arya Samaj promised to facilitate the social uplift of lower castes, its intention of enslaving untouchables to Hinduism is criticised by the Adi-Hindu leaders. Swami Acchutanand claimed in a speech, "The Samaj aimed to make all Hindus slaves of the Vedas and the Brahmins."[6]

Acchutanand and Ram Charan constructed an identity which traces out the history of the original inhabitants of India. They outlined an idealised vision of social equality and of past power and glory of the untouchables. 'Self-assertion' was an important principle of Adi-Hindu movement. Exploring the identities of self-assertion and empowerment that Adi movements espoused, Nandini Goopta states that by asserting that the untouchables were the true masters of the land, the Adi-Hindu preachers cultivated a sense of entitlement to rights and power at the same time as they heightened an awareness of historical deprivation. The stress on *atmagyan* (self-knowledge) and introspection as the source of independent knowledge without higher caste impositions also enabled the exposition of a distinction, autonomous, proud and even defiant self-identity of the untouchables.[7]

The Adi-Hindu movement provided not only 'an ideology of radical equality' and 'a strategy for doing better in every day life', but also 'a political culture for civil rights and organised protest.'[8] Though the Arya Samaj and Congress have caused to split the Adi-Hindu movement in 1930s, the Adi-Hinduism, on the whole, formed the dominant and sustained form of its political expression and a constructive identity.

Similar to the Adi movements in Punjab, Uttar Pradesh and the Namasudra movement in Bengal, the Adi movements in South India had their resonance in constructing Dalit identity. The untouchable movements in Nagpur, Adi-Dravida movement in Tamil Nadu, Adi-Karnataka movement in Mysore, Adi-Andhra movement in Andhra Pradesh under Madras Presidency and Adi-Hindu movement under the Nizam reign had paved the way for constructing the Dalit identity in South India.

In Nagpur, a relatively strong and independent Dalit movement grew and Kisan Faguji Bansode (1870-1946) was the leader of the Dalits in Nagpur. In 1903, he founded the first organisation in Mohapa, his village and many educational institutions including a school for girls in 1907. Bansode wrote several books and started several papers. Later, many leaders especially Vithoba Ravji Moonpandit (1860-1924) and Ganesh Akkaji Gavai (1888-1974) came into light as the untouchable leaders. Ganesh Akkaji Gavai founded a 'Mahar Library' and 'Mahar Sudharak Mandal' in his village. Kalicharan Nandagawali (1886-1962) founded the first girls' school and also became a member of the legislative council.

Like Acchutanand in UP and Mangoo Ram in Punjab, E.V. Rama Swamy (1879-1973) popularly known as Periyar led the self-respect movement in Tamil Nadu. One of the greatest anti-Brahman movements in India, self-respect movement targeted the Brahmin dominance criticising the idol worship. Aloysius comments on Periyar:

> His focus was not God and religion in general or in the philosophical sense but religion in particular – the Brahminical religion – taken in its practical –

social dimension of buttressing up social iniquity and in humanity."[9]

All the religions, being historical creations, tend to accumulate beliefs and practices that become anachronistic and anti-social. Periyar clarifies that:

> The self-respect movement was started with the objective of instilling a sense of self-respect in the people of this country and to unify them. The self-respect movement really endeavours in transparency, to explain why and how the people of our country had lost their self-pride, to assert that the obstacles in their way should be abolished and indeed to abolish such obstacles.[10]

Periyar educated the Dravidians and Adi-Dravidians to bring about a cultural revolt with an aim of making society casteless and egalitarian. Braj Ranjan Mani observes:

> Stressing egalitarian social relations across caste, community and gender lines, Periyar advocated the overthrow of caste and instituted non-Brahmanic forms of marriage celebrating the equality of women and her right to choose life-partner and other such practices designed to give a death blow to the Brahmanical order. Presenting a radical critique of the religious beliefs and practices in a variety of ways, Periyar wanted to demolish the whole Brahmanic structure of society which he saw as the root cause of the degradation and subordination of Women and the non-brahman populace.[11]

Periyar joined the Congress in 1919 and became a prominent figure in Tamil Congress. But soon he saw it a Brahman Tamil Congress and left it to organise the self-respect movement. Periyar also disagreed with Gandhi on issues like caste, culture and nationalism.

Another prominent identity movement in Tamil Nadu is led by Jyothee Thassay, who campaigned for education among the untouchables. He set up several schools for Dalits and his writings are remarkably modern for espousing the cause of social emancipating, Buddhism, rationalism and the new egalitarian Dravidian identity.[12] He considered the Brahmins mentally, morally and culturally depressed as they clanged on to anachronistic beliefs and obscurantist practices.

Another significant movement of identity took place in Kerala. The movements led by Ayyankali, Pokayil Yohannan and Pamapady John Joseph had a polemical role to enlighten the Dalits of Kerala. Sri Narayana Guru (1856-1928) was an active socio-political and religious reformer for nearly four decades during the most critical period of Kerala's history. He believed in the message of 'one god, one religion and one caste,' which developed a new consciousness among the Dalits. The backward caste movements in Kerala differed from other movements like that of Jotirao Phule, whose movement consisted of Shudras and Ati-Shudras (the untouchable) and women. But such an attempt was absent in Kerala and the movement lead by Sree Narayana Guru remained mostly the movement for the upliftment and empowerment of the Izhavas.

Among the Dalit movements in Kerala, the movement by Ayyankali was of great success in constructing Dalit identity. Ayyankali, an illiterate Dalit, unlike Sree Narayana Garu, was not philosophical. His movement was humanistic and democratic. To him, socio-cultural issues were more important than the economic issues. Ayyankali fought for the rights of his people to use public space and for education. By doing so, Ayyankali successfully contributed to the formation of the individual identity.

Ayyankali established open school in Vengannoor in 1904 but faced severe resistance from the caste Hindus. He gathered the scheduled castes to go on strike and continued it for one full year. To protect the strikers against criminal elements recruited by landlords, a small group of youth known as "Ayyankali Pada" was formed under his organisation. Another element that Ayyankali movement concentrated on was performing folk arts. Ayyankali collected small band of youth belonging to his caste and trained them in martial and folk arts like 'Pattukachery', 'Parijakali', 'Kolkali', Kurathiattom', 'Kakkarassi drama' and 'Valli drama.' This was his first attempt at identity construction.

Formation of 'Sadhu Jana Paripalana Sangam' (SJPS) was another significant form of identity formation in the Ayyankali movement. It was democratic in character and gender sensitive. Kerala Pulayar Maha Sabha by TT Kesava Shashtri, son-in-law of Ayyankali, obtained the four basic rights for the Dalits: right to appear in public places decently dressed, right to education, cultural rights and the right to be represented in the government. These were the subtle forms of the assertion of the Dalit identity.

The Dalit movements and literature in Andhra Pradesh began as early as 1900. The Adi-Hindu movements in Hyderabad and Adi-Dravida movement in Andhra region played significant roles in constructing the Dalit identity in the pre-independence period. The Adi-Hindu movement under Nizam rule was led by Bagya Reddy Varma (1888-1939), who organised 'Jagan Mitra Mandali' in 1906, found 'Manya Samngam' in 1911 and the Adi-Hindu organisation in the same year. Bagya Reddy Varma and his followers strongly fought for the compulsory education to the Dalit children and severely opposed the practices like child marriages, eating meat and using drink in marriages and also against the uncivic notions like 'Jogini', 'Murti' and 'Basivi' through which young and uneducated untouchable girls were devoted to gods and goddesses. Between 1906 and 1916, Bagya Reddy Varma's concentration was particularly on educating Dalits through folk songs and street plays. He went across the entire Telangana region and gave the message of revolution to the Dalits. Ariga Ramaswami and B. Syam Sundhar were other contemporaries of Bagya Reddy Varma who contributed to the construction of Dalit identity in Hyderabad state.

The Adi-Andhra Movement took place in the coastal parts of Andhra Pradesh in the Madras Presidency. The common interface between the Adi-Hindu Movement in Hyderabad and the Adi-Andhra Movement in Andhra was that both the movements were led by Bagya Reddy Varma in both the regions. The Adi-Andhra movement took place in 1917 with the 'First Provincial Panchama Mahajana Sabha' organised in Vijayawada. Bagya Reddy Varma opposed the use of the term *panchamas.* Some of the significant resolutions were: providing education to Dalit children, forming separate schools for Dalit children, allowing Dalits to use government wells, schools and public shelter, among others. The Adi-Andhra Conferences were held every year.[13]

The Adi-Andhra movement became a platform for political mobilisation. Boyi Bhimanna, Kusuma Dharmmanna and Jala Rangaswamy wrote against caste oppression, untouchability and discrimination stressing that the Dalits were the original inhabitants of the Telugu region. Gurram Jashuva's *Piradousi* (1932), *Gabbilam* (The Bat); Kusuma Dharmanna's *Nalla Dhoratham* (1933), *Harijana Chathakam* (1933), *Madhyapana Nishedham* (1930); Boyi Bhimanna's *Paleru* (1940), *Cooliraju* (1947) and *Jana Padhuni Jabhulu* (1940); Jala Rangaswami's *Mala Shuddi* (1930); Nakka China Venkataiah's *Harijana Keerthanalu* (1935);

Nuthakki Abraham and Premaiah were among those who wrote about the Dalit identity.

II

Following the mystics' and the social activists' attempts at crystallising the Dalit identity, Ambedkar (1891-1956) provided intellectual basis to the formation of the Dalit identity. Following the early Dalit movement, Ambedkar, organised Dalits socially, politically and intellectually through the process of which, the formation of the Dalit identity assumed a definitive form. Ambedkar launched many struggles during the 50 years of his social life. Ambedkar's Mahad struggle for the untouchable's access to public water in 1927 was successful as a civil rights issue. Later on he became the champion of human rights. Subsequently, Ambedkar fought for separate electorates. Ambedkar educated the Dalits that their identity is different from that of the Hindus. He even asked the Dalits to have their dwellings away from the Hindu Society. As the Chairman of the Constitution Drafting Committee and the first Law Minister, Ambedkar contributed immeasurably to the socio-cultural assertion of the Dalit identity. With the embracing of Buddhism with many of his followers and in proclaiming Buddhism as the alternative to the irrational Hinduism, Ambedkar provided spiritual basis to the Dalit identity.

Jyothiba Phule's women liberation movement inspired Ambedkar very much. Liberation of the women was taken up by him as the main part of renaissance. In addition to the Hindu reformist programmes of the widow marriages and annihilation of the *sati* system, he concentrated on education and rights for women. He struggled hard to liberate women from the age old slavery and to create a share in all the spheres of life.

While Brahma Samaj and Arya Samaj kept women in dark, Ambedkar demolished these dens and opened up new horizons of freedom and equality for women. Instead of proposing reformations for women, he put forward total liberation for women. While *Manusmruthi* enslaved women, Ambedkar awakened their mind, ignited their heart, strengthened their energies and resurrected them as powerful human beings. He fought against the state and society to realise justice for women.

The services rendered by Ambedkar to the liberation of women as a Bombay Legislature member, Law and Labour member in Viceroy's Executive Council, Indian Constitution Drafting Committee Chairman and Law Minister played important role in the enactment of laws. His relentless fight for bringing out revolutionary changes in the social and economic life of women in the form of introducing the Hindu Code Bill is important. On marriage, divorce and succession of parental properties, he proposed the abolition of polygamy and also the right of divorce to Hindu women and a share in the husband's and father's property. However, the Dalit movement in India was split into groups after Ambedkar passed away. In the subsequent period, two Dalit writer-activists Namder Dhasal and J.V. Pawar took initiative in forming the Dalit Panthers movement in Bombay in 1972. Dalit poetry, Dalit theatre (Street Plays) and Dalit autobiographies remained the direct means to address and educate the Dalits. The Dalits in India struggled for human rights. Self-assertion, self-respect and Dalit empowerment are the major themes of the movement and it imparted the proletarian radical class identity to Dalits and also linked their struggle of all oppressed people over the globe.[14]

The Dalit movements from 1980s onwards aimed at fighting for Dalit assertion. The exploitation and discrimination of the Dalits on one hand and their protest and revolt on the other hand initiated the questions of self-assertion and consciousness among the Dalits. Through their revolt, Dalits provided a new identity for them. This identity strengthened its resolve to fight every form of discrimination and determine the path for liberation. Asserting themselves, the Dalits challenged the very foundation on which the Indian society and polity are based.

III

Taking the lead from Ambedkar's theoretical basis of the Dalit identity, literary writers and activists began to narrate the Dalit experiences. Dalit writers and activists brought awareness among the Dalits. The concerns of the writers include denial of access to resources, participation in political processes, exclusion from social institutions, construction of Dalit identity, demanding equal share in resource, among others. Their writings are aimed at building awareness. Gopal guru identifies that the Dalit literature is classified into literature of Dalit cities and that of mud house writes. To him, mud house Dalit literature means writing about oral traditions of the Dalits which is ignored by the elite Dalit writers.

As Dalit writers themselves being the victims, they use literature as a vehicle to propagate the Ambedkarite ideology. The Dalit literature, that includes all the genres like short stories, novels, poetry, critical essays, plays and autobiographies, provides critical insights into the question of the Dalit identity. The teachings of Ambedkar sharpened their sensitivities, and made them outward-looking, articulate and assertive in their expression. The Dalit writings are used to educate the Dalits. The prose narratives, especially mediated between Dalit writers and the Dalits to form the modes of social protest. The dalit narratives are used to raise awareness that caste is the root cause of social discrimination. The Dalit narratives capture the local idiom finding global space. Subverting the conventional epistemology, Dalit writers challenge the Brahmanism through their writings.

The modern Dalit writing became visible with the publication of Arjun Dangle's *The Poisoned Bread* (1992) followed by Waman Nimbalkar's *Dalit Literature: Nature and Role* (2006), Sharan Kumar Limbale's *Towards an Aesthetic of Dalit Literature* (2004), Omprakash Valmiki's *Dalit Sahityaka Saundary shastra* (2001).

Though Dalit writings consist of all literary forms like poetry, short stories, songs (folklore), plays, and novels, the Dalit autobiographies seek to unveil the wretchedness and miseries which were a part of Dalit life and experience. P. Ajay Kumar, Scholar critic on Dalit studies opines that autobiographies have always been a popular form of writing because the unique experience of an individual have instructing values. He further states that the entire Dalit literature pretends to be autobiographical because Dalit writings refuse to soar high in the wings of imagination. The Dalit autobiography is understood as a genre because it adds to the growth and development of Dalit literature as a whole. The personal narratives of the Dalits speak about the heroic journey of the entire community in the process of self-assertion, liberty, self-respect and empowerment. And the same journey gives them a unique identity which is nothing but exploring the experiences of a entire people's history through narratives. Laxman Mane's *Upara* (1997), Laxman Gaikwad's *The Branded* (1998), Vasanth Moon's *Growing up Untouchable in India* (2001), Narendra Jadav's *Outcaste* (2003), Sharan Kumar Limbale's *The Outcaste* (2003), Omprakash Valmiki's *Joothan* (2003), Joseph Mackwan's *The Stepchild* (2004), Aravind Malgathi's *Government Brahmana* (2007), and of women writers Bama's *Karukku* (2000), Viramma Josiane Racine Jean Luc Racine's *Viramma: Life of a Dalit* (1997), Urmila Pawar's *The Weave of My Life* (2009) and Baby Kamble's *The Prisons We Broke* (2008) are the Dalit autobiographies in which the protagonists trace out the genesis of Dalit identity and celebrate the self of their community.

IV

Dalits' search for identity brought out a new consciousness in modern India. The Dalit identity does not merely mean identify oneself with the Dalit self, but to bring awareness among the fellow Dalits. When a Dalit narrates about himself, one does not narrate one's personal history; what one narrates is the history of his community. It is comparable to the native movements in America, native-Canadian Movement, aboriginal movements in Australia and Maori movement in New Zealand. The Durban conference on racism was an attempt at tracing out the validity of the Dalit identity in the post-modern context. However, the mainstream writers and the media belonging to the upper castes were quite indifferent: "The main stream discourse has focused by and larger on the accommodation and segregation of Dalit people into a Caste Hindu world of culture and living, a world where Dalit identity is absorbed."[15] The mainstream discourse is focused on the division of the Dalits into Hindus, Christians, Muslims and Buddhists.

Sharan Kumar Limbale depicts the resonance and interface between the Dalit movements in India and the native movements in America:

> African American and Dalit movements have proceeded along different paths and taken different turnings. But both movements are struggles for

> human rights and against exploitation...Despite differences of country, region, conditions, society and language, the similarity is the life experience of the two communities derives from the fact that both were targets of excess, injustice and slavery – their experience of pain is of a world scale...Because of these similarities, Dalit writers see the pain of African American writers as their own. African Americans have expressed their sorrow and pain through blues, ballads, stories, novels, dances and songs. Dalit writers have also communicated their pain through literature.[16]

Malcom X's *The Autobiography of Malcom X* (1965), Haarriet Beecher Stowe's *Uncle Tom's Cabin* (1852), Frantz Fanon's *Black Skin, White Masks* (1952), *The Wretched of the Earth* (1967), Ngugiwa Thiong 'o' s *A grain of Wheat* (1967), are instrumental in legitimating the Black literature and identity in the West. Their counterparts in India include Phule's *Slavery* (1873), Ambedkar's *Annihilation of Caste* (1936) and several of his writings and speeches awakened the Dalit consciousness. They are the prime resources to understand and contest the caste issues in Indian literature.

Influenced by Phule and Ambedkar many Dalit writers, who experienced the travails of caste oppression, narrated their experiences in their works. The Dalit autobiographies are found suitable for narrating their experiences. Sharan Kumar Limbale's *The Outcaste* (2003), Narendra Jadav's *Outcaste* (2003), Omprakash Valmiki's *Joothan* (2003) and Baby Kamble's *The Prisons We Broke* (2008) have been selected for examining the aspect of constructing the Dalit identity.

Identity in Dalit perspective is the similarity in terms of culture and living experiences. The experiences of caste discrimination, economic exploitation, denial of knowledge and gender dominance are common among the Dalits. The personal narratives of the Dalits deal with the problems of caste, class and gender. In this context, the language and culture of the Dalits play key role in depicting the Dalit identity. The Dalit autobiographies are written in Dalit idiom. While introducing and addressing the characters in their personal narratives, the Dalit writers use such vocabulary different from the one used by the mainstream writers. They use the pronouns 'I', 'we' and 'our' for representing Dalits and 'you', 'yours', 'they' and 'their' for addressing the non-Dalits especially the so called upper caste Hindu elites.

One of the significant characteristics of the Dalit autobiographies is that the Dalit writers never find themselves away from their community. They identify themselves within their community. Ghanshyam Shaw writes in this regard:

> Identity is concerned with the self-esteem self-image of a community – real or imaginary – dealing with the existence and role: 'who are we?' 'What position we do have in society vis-a-vis other communities?' 'How are we related to others?' Nothing standing differences in the nature of Dalit movements and the meaning of identity, there has been a common quest – the quest for equality, self-dignity and eradication of untouchability'.[17]

The self-esteem and self-image are the two key aspects of the autobiographies selected for the study: Sharan Kumar Limbale's *The Outcaste*, Narendra Jadav's *Outcaste*, Omprakash Valmiki's *Joothan* and Baby Kamble's *The Prisons We Broke.* These autobiographies depict the lives of the narrators and their people.

The narrators of the select Dalit autobiographies find their community as the protagonist of their narratives. They agree that their association with their community is inseparable and they do not dissociate themselves with their community. Sharan Kumar Limbale writes in *The Outcaste*:

> My history is my mother's life, at the most my grandmother's. My ancestry doesn't go back any further. My mother is an untouchable, while my father is a high caste from one of the privileged classes of India. Mother lives in a hut, father lives in a mansion. Father is a landlord; mother, landless. I am an *akkarmashi* (half-caste). I am condemned, branded illegitimate (Limbale, IX).[18]

Limbale raises the question of identity. He states that he was a half-breed of an upper-caste father and a Mahar mother. He deplores that his upper caste father never dares to accept Limbale as his son. Limbale states about the helpless condition of his mother who became a victim in the hands of an upper caste man. The plight of Limbale's mother is indicative of the plight of umpteen number of the Dalit women all over the country. By narrating the plight of his mother, Limbale projected a unique identity for Dalit women. G.N. Devy views:

> Limbale presents his own mother who has been cheated again and again, exploited most blatantly in every relationship she strikes, burdened with a roll call of children and upbringing. The author, however, shows a remarkable understanding of their situation. There is no cursing or blaming them in his narrative, there is not even a tone of pity for them in it."[19]

Limbale identifies himself with the Mahar community. He writes, "The umbilical cord between our locality and the village has snapped, as if the village, torn asunder, has thrown us out of it. We had grown up like aliens since our infancy. This sense of alienation increased over the years and to this day my childhood haunts me."(5) Limbale mentions about the division between the Maharwada and the village, where the Patils and other upper caste people live.

Caste discrimination and constant battle with hunger are the major themes of Limbale's autobiography. The question of identity is equally an integral part of his life story. The impossible hurdle that the author suffered his entire life was the fact that he had no identity, no home or place of belonging. His mother had once been properly married, but her husband had left her and taken their two sons. She began sleeping with the high caste men of the village. Limbale was born with a Dalit mother and a father who was the chief of a village. He could not get certain papers signed for school because he could not properly identify his caste by his mother or father, and they would not accept his grandmother as his guardian because she lived with a Muslim. When it was the time of his marriage, he could not even get married to an outcaste girl because his blood was not pure. He realised that he was not wanted anywhere. Eventually, a drunkard who had offered Limbale his daughter would not allow her to leave after the wedding because of Limbale's background. The clouds of doubt and identity hung over this poor outcaste boy throughout his life.

However, in several acts of incredible strength and bravery, he did not allow these socially constructed obstacles to stop him from being educated. He realised the depth of division caused by the conflict between Hindus and Muslims. Limbale states that the influence of Ambedkar and his involvement in the Dalit Panthers movement changed his life. Tromila Wheat writes:

Limbale's autobiography is a good quick read that would interest any students taking a course on modern India. It is an objective work that shows little bitterness or remorse. The author includes an excellent introduction that introduces the caste system to the Western reader. We can experience the humiliation of the Dalit community at the hands of an unthinking privileged class and the hopelessness of the situation of people born in lower castes."[20]

Narendra Jadav identifies himself with the people to whom he belongs to in his *Outcaste* (2003). Irrespective of the qualification he acquired and the position he reached, he could not stop himself finding among his community people. Jadav writes:

> These people, raw, down-to-earth, unpolished are the ones to whom I belong", I thought. Born in the confines of poverty, illiteracy and ignorance they were at different stages of struggles in life. But they are my people, I thought, with a sense of belonging, as they looked at me with awe. In their eyes, I had managed, through hard work and perseverance to climb out of the morass of untouchability, illiteracy and backwardness." (Jadav, 203)[21]

The expressions like 'the one to whom I belong' and 'but they are my people' imply that Jadav always identifies himself with his community. Jadav states that no matter what he did, where he went, or what success he achieved, he would always be looked upon as a Mahar, an untouchable. Jadav's argument is suggestive of the caste identity irrespective of the place, position and success. Jadav writes further: "It is unfortunate truth of our society that whatever height a man might scale, his caste is never cast off; it remains an inseparable part of his identity. His caste always remains a cause for scorn or contempt. Only the type of humiliation changes." (208)

Om Prakash Valmiki depicts in *Joothan* (2003) the identity of the Dalits based on caste. He shows the difference between the Chuhras to whom Valmiki belongs and that of the Tagas, the upper caste people. *Joothan* begins with the discrimination of Barla village:

> Our house was adjacent to Chandrabhan Taga's gher or cowshed. Next to it lived the families of Muslim weavers. Right in front of Chandrabhan Taga's gher was a little johri, a pond, which had created a sort of partition between the Chuhras dwelling and the village ... on one side of the pit were the high walls of the brick homes of the tagas...on the edges of the pond were the homes of the Chuhras... (Valmiki, 1)[22]

Similar to Sharan Kumar Limbale's autobiography, Valmiki's autobiography also had identical line of caste divisions in the villages between the upper caste and the Dalits.

Valmiki writes that "the pigs wandering in narrow lanes, naked children, dogs, daily fights, this was the environment of my childhood."(1) Valmiki's argument is a critique of Gandhian notion of the village and the *Gram Swarajyam*. The Chuhras have to work without pay. Valmiki writes:

> We did all sorts of work for the Tagas, including cleaning, agricultural work and general labour. We would often have to work without pay. Nobody dared to refuge this unpaid work for which we got neither money nor grain. Instead, we got sworn at and abused.(2)

The untouchables in villages were forced to undertake unpaid work. In this context, Valmiki identifies himself with his caste people. Regarding the identity of the Dalits by names, he writes: "They did not call us by our names. If a person were older, then he would be called "Oe Chuhre." If the person was younger or of the same age, then 'Abey Chuhre' was used."(2) The relative pronoun 'us' and the possessive pronoun 'our' imply that Valmiki identifies himself with his Chuhra community like Limbale and Jadav identified with their Mahar community.

> Valmiki is equally concerned about the Dalit issues. Substantiating the contribution of Valmiki in representing the Chuhra community, Raj Kumar writes: "He is convinced that only by raising caste-related issues he will be able to start a discussion on the plight of Dalits at a national level. The publication of *Joothan* in English in the meantime has generated a lot of discussion related to Dalits. Valmiki announces that the main issue of his autobiography is about 'identity' concerning caste."[23] Though the title *Joothan – A Dalit's Life* indicates that it is about the life story of an individual, it speaks about the history of the entire Chuhra community. The Chuhra community has been subjected to the caste-based discrimination for ages. Valmiki describes how his entire community depends on the leftover food thrown out by the upper castes in return for their hard but unpaid work. The entire community had to depend on the mercy of the upper castes who, instead of paying labour, exploit them.

Valmiki dispensed with the practice of begging *Salam,* a begging tradition of the Chuhras even at an early age. Though Valmiki faced humiliation and insults from both upper caste teachers and students in school and college life, he never suppressed his desire to continue with his studies. Due to his hard work and determination, he became the first graduate in his community. He inspired his caste people to join their children in schools. Valmiki developed the Dalit consciousness among his people. He could do so because of his understanding of the philosophy of Dr Ambedkar. Raj Kumar writes:

> He is pained to see his fellow community members doing the same traditional duties without any protest. By writing his autobiography Valmiki thus renders a great service to his community. Along with his life-history he also narrates the painful experiences of his community life. It is in this sense that Valmiki's life-story is also the story of his community."[24]

Valmiki is one among the committed Dalit writers determined to bring awareness among his people.

Baby Kamble's *The Prisons We Broke* (2008) is a Dalit woman's autobiography. Though written by a woman, it deals with the identity of the Dalit community in general. Kamble states in an interview:

> Well, I wrote about what my community experienced. The suffering of my people became my own suffering. Their experiences become mine. So I really find it very difficult to think of myself outside of my community."(Kamble, 205)[25]

Kamble's determination to identify herself with her community is worth commending. She writes about the poor and the helpless conditions of her people. She writes that the Dalits were treated like animals. They were reduced to a condition worse than that of the bullocks kept in the courtyards of the high castes:

> The bullocks were at least given some dry grass to eat. The bullocks ate the grass and slogged for their masters. But we were merely given leftovers. We ate the leftovers without complaining and laboured for others. The only difference, however, was that the

> beasts could eat a bellyful and they could stay in their masters courtyards. But our condition was far worse, our place was in the garbage pits outside the village, where everyone threw away their waste. That was where we lived in our poor huts, amidst all the filth! (49)

Kamble's autobiography deals with three major problems of the society: firstly, the oppression and exploitation of the Dalit by the upper class: secondly, the discrimination towards women in a patriarchal society and finally the influence of Dr Ambedkar on the narrator. Poverty was an unresolved problem among the Mahars and the condition of the Mahar women was miserable. The Dalits are denied access to public space and resources. Though the narrator was discriminated against by the upper caste teachers and students, she was resilient in facing them. She says that she could do so because of the influence of Ambedkar on her. According to her, Ambedkar was the light of Dalits' life. He asked the Mahars to educate their children, and inspired them to fight against the atrocities. He asked them not to give offerings to the gods who never cared about them. And he also asked them not to eat the meat of the dead animals.[26]

The Dalit autobiographer in general identifies himself/herself within the community. Besides, the aspects of self-assertion, self-respect and building Dalit consciousness are the central concerns of a Dalit autobiography. Political consciousness among the Dalits is another major concern of the texts. Though the authors of the Dalit autobiographies suffer from unique problems, the philosophy of Ambedkar is considered the appropriate remedy for the liberation of the Dalits. In other words, the life and philosophy has been the basis of the formation and construction of the Dalit identity.

Therefore the protagonists of the autobiographies use education as the true weapon for the emancipation of the Dalits.

Badri Narayan opines that the Dalit narratives are the narratives of identity and self-respect: "The new narratives of the Dalit politics, which appear as cultural narratives of identity and self-respect are filled with memories of dissent against dominance and oppression."[27] The Dalit narratives are written in the respective Dalit idiom. The construction of the Dalit narratives is based on a sense of self-respect. Badri Narayan writes:

> Dalits, for acquiring social respect, use their personal narratives through which they glorify their community. The identity created through their narratives of the past by the Dalits renders instable the canons determined by Brahmanism for granting status in society, such as purity-pollution beliefs, birth-based ascription, specific caste characterisation and caste hierarchy, and status ascription.[28]

'Dalit consciousness' refers to the Dalit politics and identity in terms of political awareness and the notion of collective identity among the diverse Dalit communities. These two uses are fundamentally the same in their emphasis on the need to be aware of the exploitation based on caste. Narendra Jadav's *Out Caste* is about the journey of a Dalit family from a small village, Ozar, to a big city Mumbai, and then to far off places like the USA. It presents the story of a Dalit family in search of Dalit dignity. It depicts the oppressive and exploitative village life as well as the successes of the three generations of this family. The central narrative follows the transformation of this family. It was the great transformation of Jadav's family into a very successful family of eminent scholars and officers.

In the foregoing discussion, an attempt has been made to delineate the various identity movements in historical outline. The non-Brahmin movements in India, beginning from the Bhakti period to the contemporary period, contributed to the process of constructing alternative history against the caste Hindus. It has been argued in the chapter that the construction of the Dalit identity is not a contemporary feature. The attempts of the identity movements of the early period have been obliterated. The Dalit autobiographies selected for the study have been interpreted as the attempts of relocating, reforming and reconstructing the Dalit identity as a challenge to the Brahminical oppressive social order.

References

1. Braj Ranjan Mari, *Debrahmanising History : Dominance and Resistance in Indian Society,* New Delhi : Monetary, 2005, 168-69.

2. Gail Omvedt, Dalit Visions: *The Anti-Caste Movement and the Construction of an Indian Identity,* New Delhi : Orient Longman, 2006, 34.

3. Bharat Patankar and Gail Omvedt, *The Dalit Liberation Movement in Colonial Period,* New Delhi: Critical Quest, 2007, 13.

4. Sekhar Bandyopadlay, *The Namasudra Movement*, New Delhi : Critical Quest, 2005, 3.

5. Ronki Ram Manguo Ram, *Ad Dharm and The Dalit Movement in Punjab*, New Delhi : Critical Quest, 2008, 9.

6. Nandini Goopt, *Swami Acchutanand and The Adi-Hindu Movement,* New Delhi: Critical Quest, 2006, 13.

7. Nandini Goopt, 21.

8. R. S. Khare, *The Untouchable as Himself : Ideology, Identity and Pragmatism among the Lucknow Chamars,* Cambridge, 1984, 78.

9. Aloysius, G., *Periyar on Islam*, New Delhi: Critical Quest, 2004, 4.

10. Aloysius, G., 5.

11. Braj Ranjan Mani, *Debrahmanising History: Dominance and Resistance in Indian Society,* New Delhi: Manohar, 2007, 324-25.

12. Braj Ranjan Mani, 314.

13. Gail Omvedt, *Dalits and Democratic Revolution: Dr Ambedkar and the Dalit Movement in Colonial India,* New Delhi: Sage, 1994, 118.

14. Anand Teltumde, *Ambedkar for the Post-Ambedkar Dalit Movement,* Pune: Sugawa Prakashan, 1997, 16.

15. Rajesh Kumar, *Contestation and Negotiation of Dalit Identities: A Perspective from Below*, (http;// findarticles.com/ p/ articles/mi7018/is_1_33/ai_n28438652)

16. Sharan Kumar Limbale, *Towards an Aesthetic of Dalit Literature,* New Delhi: Orient Longman, 2007, 86-87.

17. Ghanshyam Shaw, *Dalit Identity and Politics*, Delhi: Sage, 195.

18. Sharan Kumar Limbale, *The Outcaste*, New Delhi: Orient Longman, 2003, ix. (Subsequent references to this addition with page numbers are given in parenthesis).

19. Sharan Kumar Limbale, XXV-VI.

20. Thromila Wheat, 2, (http://findarticles.com/p/articles/mi 7066/ is 27/ai n28320861.)

21. Narendra Jadav, *Out Caste*, New Delhi: Viking, 2003, 206. (Subsequent references to this addition with page numbers are given in parenthesis).

22. Omprakash Valmiki, *Joothan- A Dalit's Life*, Kolkata: Samya, 2003,1. (Subsequent references to this addition with page numbers are given in parenthesis).

23. Raj Kumar, *Dalit Personal Narratives: Reading Caste, Nation and Identity*, New Delhi: Orient Longman, 2010, 197.

24. Raj Kumar, 197.

25. Baby Kamble, *The Prisons We Broke*, New Delhi: Orient Longman, 2008, 136. (Subsequent references to this addition with page numbers are given in parenthesis).

26. <http://out-caste.blogspot.com/2008/03/prisons-we-broke-baby-kamble.html>

27. Badri Narayan, *Women Heroes and Dalit Assertion in North India*, New Delhi: Sage, 2006, 40.

28. Badri Narayan, 95.

6

Conclusion

In this dissertation entitled, “Writing the Self: A Thematic Study of Dalit Autobiographies,” an attempt has been made to examine four Dalit autobiographies that include Sharan Kumar Limbale’s *The Out Caste* (2003), Narendra Jadav’s *Outcaste* (2003), Omprakash Valmiki’s *Joothan* (2003) and Baby Kamble’s *The Prisons We Broke* (2008). The study, being thematic in approach, has been divided into six chapters. The Introductory chapter, “Contextualising Autobiography: Writing for the Community” traced the evolution of the autobiography in the Indian context in general and the Dalit autobiographies in particular. The chapter explored the impact of the contemporary Dalit movements, politics and assertion. The historical need for documenting the Dalit experiences in the form of the Dalit autobiographies has been accounted for. The focus of the chapter has been that the nationalist ideology has been interrogated by the Dalit theoreticians and activists, and the genre of the Dalit autobiography reinforces the need for countering the Brahminical hegemony.

The second chapter, “Denial of Education: Subverting the Monopoly” attempted to examine the aspect of the denial of education to the Dalits as delineated in select autobiographies. The tradition of the Indian education, essentially being exclusivist, distanced a majority of the social groups from education. The tradition of the denial of education continues even in the modern and secular educational system. This chapter explored how the Brahminical system of exclusivist pedagogy made the Dalits undergo the experience of insult, humiliation, psychological and physical violence and ultimately a sense of alienation from the mainstream society. However, it has been argued in the chapter that the Dalits challenged their exclusion from education, and came out of what may be termed the 'Dronacharya syndrome.' The Dalits used the denial of education to their advantage, and accomplished in the fields of education. The autobiographies of Limbale, Jadav, Valmiki and Kamble have been illustrated as to how the protagonists overcame the hurdles so as to excel themselves in education and career.

The third chapter, "Experiencing Discrimination: Dalit Livid Lives" delineated different aspects of humiliation and social exclusion at different spheres of life. The chapter explored how the Dalits are historically forced to accept the social, religious and economic exclusion. The thrust of the chapter has been to explore how the Dalit writers engage with caste as a subjective category of how they lived and experienced. The study also focused on how the Dalit autobiographies mapped the nuanced and unnoticed pains of the Dalits experience of discrimination.

The fourth chapter, "Writing Dalit Gender: Dalit among Dalits" dealt with the revisiting and redefinition of the Dalit women's experience of caste and gender discrimination. The chapter focused on how the Dalit women experience double alienation related to caste and gender. The chapter illustrated the sociological conditions that characterise the Dalit women as the downtrodden of the downtrodden. The discrimination of the Dalit women and their struggles for emancipation has been interpreted in terms of Ambedkar's theory of asserting the self.

The fifth chapter, "Construction of Dalit Identity: Assertion of the Self" primarily dealt with the legacy of the Bhakti movement, the Adi movements and Ambedkar's contribution to the formulation of an alternative egalitarian, secular and modern identity for the Dalits. The chapter focused on non-Brahman movements during the colonial India, which questioned the Brahmin dominance in the socio-cultural and religious spheres. The chapter examined the aspect of how the non-Brahmin movements were suppressed and obliterated by the discourse of Gandhian '*Ramarajya*' and Nehruvian 'Secularism.' The formation of the Dalit identity was based on giving a unique political identity through active participation in the process of making a modern, democratic and secular India. The chapter focused on how the Dalit autobiographies are considered historical documentations of self-assertion, self-respect, liberation and empowerment of the Dalits.

Having summed up the study, the concluding Chapter presents the findings of the research as follows:

(a) Quest for identity is an important aspect of the Dalit autobiographies, which represent the struggles of the Dalits for social equality and justice. The Dalit autobiographies in general are the narratives of the caste history of the Dalits. In the process of writing their caste history, the narrators interrogate the mainstream culture, religion, polity and the bases of exploitation. In so doing, the Dalit narratives construct an alternative history by liberally drawing from their culture, language and myth.

(b) The Dalit autobiographies, by relocating, redefining and reconstructing the Dalit identity, demand for the legitimacy of the due space in history, culture, literature, economy and politics. The Dalit writers interrogate the mainstream autobiographies: "Gandhi, Nehru and Chauduri individually represent different world views, but socio-culturally they belong to a common category, i.e., they were upper caste men and hence they were quite privileged to have an audience worldwide...In recent times, there have been a considerable number of crucial studies on Indian upper caste women's autobiographies."[1]

(c) The Dalit autobiographies do not share the features of the mainstream autobiographies. Influenced by Ambedkar, the authors of the Dalit autobiographies deal with the aspect of asserting the Dalit self, which in turn is aimed at the liberation of the Dalits. The philosophy of Ambedkar brought a new consciousness among the Dalits. The consciousness about their exploitation, atrocities and injustice experienced by the Dalits help them in shaping their intellectual life.

(d) Though the Dalit autobiographies are full of agony and angst, they are aimed at awakening the Dalits and raising their consciousness. The Dalit autobiographies are not merely the writings of vengeance to spread hatred against the caste Hindus but also to promote the heritage of the Dalits. The Dalit autobiographies are aimed at rebuilding society to promote honour, dignity, justice and equality. The subjectivity of the Dalit autobiographies needs to be understood in terms of the communal self: "The identity of a person will be based on the location to which he/she belongs. Accordingly, the person will undergo the experiences in life. In order to understand the life-experiences of a person several disparate identical criterion can be put to test. It can be caste, class, ethnicity, language, religion, region, gender etc."[2]

(e) The very emergence of the Dalit autobiography is a form of the Dalit resistance because Dalits are using this opportunity to assert their identities through their writings. The growing number of Dalit autobiographies is a clear instance of how Dalits have been breaking the traditional silence.

The study, however, is not without limitations. The aspect of writing the self has been carried out by selecting four Dalit autobiographies as the primary sources. Though there are a number of Dalit autobiographies available in English translations, the researcher confined the work to the select four autobiographies as examining all the works is likely to be unwieldy. There is a scope of examining, in further research, the remaining autobiographies for exploring the Dalit self.

References

1. Raj Kumar, *Dalit Personal Narratives: Reading Caste, Nation and Gender*, New Delhi: Orient Longman, 2010, 1.

2. Raj Kumar, 3.

Bibliography

PRIMARY SOURCES:

Jadhav, Narendra. *Outcaste: A Memoir.* New Delhi: Viking, 2003.

Kamble, Baby. *The Prisons We Broke.* Translated from Marathi by Maya Pandit. Chennai: Orient Longman, 2008.

Limbale, Sharankumar. *The Outcaste.* Translated from Marathi by Santosh Bhoomkar. New Delhi: Oxford University Press, 2003.

Valmiki, Omprakash. *Joothan: A Dalit's Life.* Translated from Hindi by Arun Prabha Mukherjee. Calcutta: Samya, 2003.

SECONDARY SOURCES:

Agnivesh, Swami and Thampu, Valson. "Discrimination that must be Cast Away," in *Caste, Race and Discrimination: Discourses in International Context* Edited by Sukhadeo Thorat and Umakanth. New Delhi, Rawat Publications, 2004.

Allen Douglas (ed). *Culture and Self: Philosophical and Religious Perspectives, East and West.* U.S.A.: Westview Press, 1997.

Aloysius, G. *Nationalism without a Nation in India.* New Delhi: Oxford University Press, 1997.

Aloysius, G. *Religion as Emancipatory Identity: A Buddhist Movement of the Tamils under Colonialism.* New Delhi: New Age International Publishers, 1998.

———. *Periyar on Islam.* New Delhi: Critical Quest, 2004.

———. *Interpreting Kerala's Social Development.* New Delhi: Critical Quest, 2005.

———. *Dalit Subaltern Emergence in Region Cultural Subjectivity: Iyothee Thassar and Emancipatory Buddhism.* New Delhi: Critical Quest, 2007.

Ambedkar, B. R. *What Congress and Gandhi have done for Untouchables.* Bombay: Thacker and Co., 1945.

———. *The Untouchables: Who are they? And why they became Untouchables!* New Delhi: Amrit Book, 1948.

Anand, Mulk Raj. *Apology for Heroism: A Brief Autobiography of Ideas (1946).*New Delhi: Arnold Heinemann, 1986.

———. *Untouchable* (1935) New Delhi: Arnold Publishers, 1981.

———. and Zelliot, Eleanor. *An Anthology of Dalit Literature* (Poems). New Delhi: Gyan Publishing House, 1992.

Anand, S. *Touchable Tales: Publishing and Reading Dalit Literature.* Pondicherry: Navayana, 2003.

Anand, Tellumbale. *Ambedkar for the Post-Ambedkar Dalit Movement.* Pune: Sugawa Prakashan, 1997.

Anderson, Linda. *Women and Autobiography in the Twentieth Century.* Great Britain: Prentice Hall, 1997.

———. *Autobiography.* London: Routledge, 2001.

Ashley, Kathleen (ed). *Autobiography and Post-Modernism.* Boston: The University of Massachusetts Press, 1994.

Baisantry, D. K. *Ambedkar: The Total Revolutionary.* New Delhi: Segment Book Distributors, 1991.

Bama, *Karukku* (1992). Translated from Tamil by Lakshmi Holmstrom. Chennai: Macmillan, 2000.

———. *Sangati* (1994). Translated from Tamil by Lakshmi Holmstrom. New Delhi: Oxford University Press, 2005.

———. *Vanamam-Vendetta.* Translated from Tamil by Lakshmi Holmstrom. New Delhi: Oxford University Press, 2008.

Bandyopadhay, Sekhar. *The Namasudra Movement.* New Delhi: Critical Quest, 2005.

Banerjea, Surendranath. *A Nation in Making: Being the Reminiscences of Fifty Years of Public Life.* Madras: Oxford University Press, 1925.

Barry, Peter. *Beginning Theory: An Introduction to Literary and Cultural Theory.* New Delhi, Viva, 2008.

Basu, Tapan (ed). *Translating Caste.* New Delhi: Katha, 2002.

Bayly, Susan. *Caste, Society and Politics in India: From the Eighteenth Century to the Modern Age. The New Cambridge History of India.* Vol. IV. Cambridge: Cambridge University Press, 1979.

Beauvoir, Simone de. *The Second Sex* (1949). Translated and edited by H.M. Parshley. London: Vintage, 1997.

Beteille, Andre. *Caste: Old and New.* Delhi: Oxford University Press, 1969.

Beteille, Andre. *Equality among Men.* Delhi: Oxford University Press, 1977.

———. *Equality and Inequality: Theory and Practice.* Delhi: Oxford University Press, 1983.

Beth, Sarah. Dalit autobiographies in Hindi: The Transformation of Pain into Resistance. www.sanet.lu.so./EASASpapers/4Sarah Beth.pdf.

Bhargava, Deepali. *Manu Smriti: A Sociological Analysis.* Jaipur: Rawat Publications, 1989.

Bhave, Sumitra. *Pan on Fire.* Translated by Gauri Deshpande. New Delhi: Indian Social Institute, 1988.

Billington, Mary Frances. *Women in India.* New Delhi: Amarko Book Agency, 1973.

Blanchard, Marc Eli. "The Critique of Autobiography". *Comparative Literature.* Vol. 34, No. 2. Eugene: University of Oregon, Spring 1982.

Bose, Subhas Chandra. *An Indian Pilgrim or Autobiography of Subhas Chandra Bose* (1897-1920). Part I. Calcutta: Thacker and Spinh, 1948.

Bowles, Gloria and Klein, Duelli (eds). *Theories of Women Studies.* London: Routledge and Kegan Paul, 1983.

Broadzki, Balla and Schenck, Celeste (eds). *Life / Lines: Theorizing Women's Autobiography.* Ithaca: Cornell University Press, 1988.

Burr, Anna Robeson. *The Autobiography: A Critical and Comparative Study.* New York: Houghton Mifflin, 1958.

Castells, M. *The Power of Identity.* Oxford: Blackwell, 1997.

Chakravarthi, Uma. *Rewriting History: The Life and Times of Pandita Ramabai.* Delhi: Kali for Women, 1998.

———. *Gendering Caste through a Feminist Lens.* Calcutta: Stree 2006.

Chandorkar, Leena. *Eye Me Myself: A Study of Six Women's Autobiographies.* Delhi: New Century Publications, 2002.

Chatterjee, Searle and Sharma, Ursula. *Contextualising Caste: Post-Dumortian Approaches.* U.K.: Blackwell Publishers, 1994.

Chatterji, Soma A. *The Indian Women's Search for an Identity* (1998). New Delhi: Vikash Publishing House Pvt. Ltd., 1997.

Chaubisa, M. L. *Caste, Tribe and Exploitation.* Udaipur: Himansu Publications, 1988.

Chaudhuri, Maitraye (ed). *Feminism in India: Issues in Contemporary Indian Feminism.* New Delhi: Kali for Women, 2004.

Chaudhuri, Nirad C. *The Autobiography of an Unknown Indian* (1951). Bombay: Jaico Publishing House, 1994.

Chinna Rao, Yagati. *Dalits Struggle for Identity,* 2003. Hyderabad: Hyderabad Book Trust, 2008.

Choudhuri, Ramadevi. *Jiwan Pathe* (1984). Translated as *Into the Sun: An Autobiography* by Manmohan Choudhuri. New Delhi: National Gandhi Museum, 1998.

Clark, Romy and Ivanic, Roz. *The Politics of Writing.* London: Routledge, 1997.

Cockshut, A. O. J. *The Art of Autobiography in 19th and 20th Century England.* New Haven: Yale University Press, 1984.

Coomaraswamy, Anand K. *Hinduism and Buddhism.* Delhi: Munshiram Manoharlal Publishers, 1975.

Crowley, Helen and Himmelweet, Susan (eds). *Knowing Women: Feminism and Knowledge.* U.K.: Polity Press, 1992.

Currie, Mark. *Postmodern Narrative Theory.* London: Macmillan, 1998.

Curthoys, Ann. "Adventures of Feminism: Simone de Beauvoir's Autobiographies, Women's Liberation, and Self-Fashioning". *Feminist Review.* No. 64. Spring, 2000.

Dangle, Arjun (ed). *Poisoned Bread: Translation from Modern Marathi Dalit Literature* (1992). Bombay: Orient Longman, 1994.

Das, Bhagwan and Massey, James. *Dalit Solidarity.* Delhi: ISPCK, 1995.

Das, Bijaya Kumar. *Postmodern Indian English Literature.* New Delhi: Atlantic Publishers, 2003.

Das, D. P. *The Untouchable Story.* Delhi: Allied Publishers, 1985.

Das, Kamala. *My Story.* New Delhi: Sterling Publishers, 1976.

Dasi, Binodini. *My Story* and *My Life as an Actress.* Translated and edited by Rimli Bhattacharya. New Delhi: Kali for Women, 1989.

Day, Lal Behari. *Bengal Peasant Life (Govind Samanta); Folk Tales of Bengal; Recollections of My School Days* edited by Mahadev Prasad Saha. Calcutta: Indian Editions, 1969.

Delany, Paul. *British Autobiography in the 17th Century.* London: Routledge, 1969.

Desai, Morarji. *The Story of My Life.* Vols. I-III. Bombay: Macmillan, 1974-79.

Deshmukh, C. D. *The Source of My Life.* Bombay: Orient Longman, 1975.

Devi, Gayatri. *A Princess Remembers: The Memoirs of the Maharani of Jaipur.* New Delhi: Rupa, 1999.

Dhavan, Rajeev. "India's Apartheid," in *Caste, Race and Discrimination: Discourses in International Context,* Edited by Sukhadeo Thorat and Umakanth. New Delhi, Rawat Publications, 2004.

Douglass, Frederick. *Narrative of the Life of Frederick Douglass, an American Slave. Written by Himself.* (1982). Edited by Houston A. Baker, Jr. New York: Penguin Books, 1986.

Dube, Saurabh. *Untouchable Pasts: Religion, Identity and Power among a Central Indian Community,* (1950-1980). Albany: State University of New York Press, 1998.

Dumont, Louis. *Homo Hierarchichus: The Caste System and Its Implication.* Chicago: University of Chicago Press, 1980.

Eagleton, Mary (ed). *Feminist Literary Theory: A Reader.* Oxford: Blackwell, 1995.

Elbaz, Robert. *The Changing Nature of the Self: A Critical Study of the Autobiographic Discourse.* London: Croom Helm, 1988.

Felski, Rita. *Beyond Feminist Aesthetics: Feminist Literature and Social Change.* London: Hutchinson Radius, 1989.

Fernandes, Walter. *The Emerging Dalit Identity: The Re-assertion of the Subalterns* (ed). New Delhi: Indian Social Institute, 1996.

Forrester, Dunkan B. *Caste and Christianity.* London: Carion Press, 1980.

Foucault, Michael. "What is an Author?" Translated by James Venit. *Partisan Review,* Prague: Prague University Press, Autumn, 1974.

———. *Power/Knowledge,* Edited by Rabinow Paul, New York: Peregrine, 1984.

———."Writing the Self". Translated by Ann Hobart in *Foucault and His Interlocutors.* Edited by Arnold J. Davidson. Chicago: Chicago Press, 1997.

Franco, Fernando (ed). *Pain and Awakening: The Dynamics of Dalit Identity in Bihar.* Gujarat and Uttar Pradesh, New Delhi: Indian Social Institute, 2002.

———*(et al). Journeys to Freedom: Dalit Narratives.* Calcutta: Samya, 2004.

Freeman, James M. *Untouchable: An Indian Life History.* London: George Allen and Unwin, 1979.

Frieden, Sandra. *Autobiography: Self into Form. German-Language Autobiographical Writings of the 1970s.* Frankfurt: Verlag Peterlang, 1983.

Gaikwad, Laxman. *Uchalya.* Translated as *The Branded* by P. A. Kolharkar. New Delhi: Sahitya Akademi, 1998.

Gandhi, M. K. *Hindu Dharma* (1978). New Delhi: Orient Paperbacks, 1991.

———. *An Autobiography or the Story of My Experiments with Truth* (1927). Ahmedabad: Navjivan Publishing House, 1993.

Geetha, V. and Rajadurai, S. V. *Towards a Non-Brahmin Millennium.* Calcutta: Samya, 1998.

Ghardially, Rehana. *Women in Indian Society*. New Delhi: Sage Publications, 1988.

Ghose, Shankar. *The Western Impact in Indian Politics*. New Delhi: Allied Publishers, 1967.

Ghurye, G. S. *Caste and Class in India*. Bombay: Popular Prakashan, 1957.

Gilmore, Leigh. *Autobiographies: A Feminist Theory of Women's Self-representation*. Ithaca and London: Cornell University Press, 1994.

Gokhale, Jayashree. *From Confessions to Confrontation: The Politics of an Indian Untouchable Community*. Bombay: Popular Prakashan, 1993.

Goopt, Nandini. *Swami Acchutanand and The Adi-Hindu Movement*. New Delhi: Critical Quest, 2006.

Gopalan, A. K. *In the Cause of the People: Reminiscences*. Madras: Orient Longman, 1973.

Gorky, Maxim. *My Apprenticeship. My Universities*. Moscow: Progress Publishers, 1976.

———. *Childhood* (1954). Translated by Margaret Wettlin. Moscow: Raduga Publishers, 1990.

Goswami, Indira. *An Unfinished Autobiography* (1986). Translated by P. Kotoky. New Delhi: Sterling Publishers, 2002.

Gould, Harold A. *The Hindu Caste System*. Delhi: Chanakya Publications, 1987.

Green, Gayle and Khan, Coppelia (eds). *Changing Subject: The Making of Feminist Literary Criticism*. London: Routledge, 1993.

Guha, Ranjit. *A Subaltern Studies Reader:* 1986-1995. Delhi: Oxford University Press, 1998.

Guru, Gopal. "*Joothan: A Dalits Life* by Omprakash Valmiki" (Review). *Seminar.* No. 530, 2003.

———."Afterward" in *The Prisons We Broke.* New Delhi: Orient Black Swan, 2008.

Hanlon, Rosalind. *Caste, Conflict and Ideology.* London: Cambridge University Press, 1985.

Harish, Ranjana. *Indian Women's Autobiography.* New Delhi: Arnold Publishers, 1993.

——. *The Female Footprints.* New Delhi: Sterling Publishers, 1996.

Hazari. *Untouchable: The Autobiography of an Indian Outcaste.* New York: Praeger Publishers, 1970.

Herrera, Nancy Cooke de. *Beyond Gurus: A Woman of Many Worlds.* New Delhi: Rupa, 1994.

Hesse, Hermann. *Autobiographical Writings.* Translated by Denver Lindley. London: Triad/Panther Books, 1985.

Hidayatullah, M. *My Own Boswell.* New Delhi: Arnold-Heinemann,1980.

Hitler, Adolf. *Mein Kampf. (My Struggle).* Bombay: Jaico, 1988.

Holbrook, David. *Images of Women in Literature.* New York: New York University Press, 1989.

Ilaiah, Kancha. *Why I am not a Hindu.* Kolkata: Samya, 1996.

——. *God as Political Philosopher: Buddha's Challenge to Brahmanism.* Kolkata: Samya, 2004.

Isaacs, Harold R. *India's Ex-Untouchables.* Bombay: Asia Publishing House, 1965.

Iyengar, A. S. *All Through the Gandhian Era.* Bombay: Hind Kitabs, 1950.

Jain, Jasbir. *Writing Women across Cultures.* Jaipur and New Delhi: Rawat Publications, 2002.

Jaipal, Rikhi. *Memories of a Half Life and Flowers of Grass.* New Delhi: Allied Publishers, 1991.

Jangam, Chinnaih. *Dilemmas of Dalit Agendas: Political Subjugation and Self Emancipation in Telugu Country 1910-1950.* Dalit Conference, December 3-05, 2008, Philadelphia, University of Pennsylvania.

Jatav, D. R. *A Silent Soldier: An Autobiography.* Jaipur: Samata Sahitya Sadan, 2000.

Jayakar, M. R. *The Story of My Life.* Vols. I and II. Bombay: Asia Publishing House, 1958 and 1959.

Jelinek, Estelle C. *The Tradition of Women's Autobiography: From Antiquity to the Present.* Boston: Twayne Publishers, 1986.

Jeyaram, N. and Saberwal, S. (eds). *Social Conflicts.* Oxford: Oxford University Press, 1996.

Jodhka, Surinder S. "Community and Identities: Interrogating Contemporary Discourses on India". *Economic and Political Weekly.* Vol. XXXIV. No.41. October 9, 1999.

Jogdand, P. G. *Dalit Movement in Maharashtra.* New Delhi: Kanak Publications, 1991.

——(ed). *Dalit Women in India: Issues and Perspective.* New Delhi: Gyan Publishing House, 1996.

Johnson, Hazel and Bernsted (eds). *Third World Lives of Struggle.* Oxford: Heineman, 1982.

Joshi, Barbara (ed). *Untouchable: Voices of the Dalit Liberation Movement.* New Delhi: Select Book Service Syndicate, 1986.

Josiane Racine and Jean-Luce Racine, *Viramma: Life of an Untouchable.* Translated by Will Hobson. Paris: Verso, 1997.

Jung, Annes. *Breaking the Silence: Voices of Women from Around the World.* New Delhi: Viking and Unesco Publishing, 1997.

Kakar, Sudhir (ed). *Identity and Adulthood* (1979) Delhi: Oxford University Press, 1993.

Kalhana. *Rajatarangini: A Chronicle of the Kings of Kashmir.* Translated by M. A. Stein. Vols. I and II. Delhi: Motilal Banarasidass, 1961.

Kamble, Shantabai. *Majya Jalmachi Chittarkatha* (Marathi). Pune: Suguva Prakashan, 1990.

Kannabiran, K.G. "We, the Other People," in *Caste, Race and Discrimination: Discourses in International Context,* Edited by Sukhadeo Thorat and Umakanth New Delhi, Rawat Publications, 2004.

Kasturi, Leela and Mazumdar, Vina (eds). *Women and Indian Nationalism.* New Delhi: Vikas Publishing House, 1994.

Kaul, B. M. *The Untold Story.* Bombay: Allied Publishers, 1967.

Kaul, T. N. *Reminiscences: Discreet and Indiscreet.* New Delhi: Lancers Publishers, 1982.

Kelly, Joan. *Women, History and Theory* (1984). London: The University of Chicago Press, 1986.

Khare, R. S. *The Untouchable as Himself: Ideology, Identity and Pragmatism among the Lucknow Chamars.* New Delhi, Cambridge, 1984.

Krishna, Mudaliyar A. Bala. *The Reminiscences of a Retired Hindu Official.* Madras: Commercial Press, 1905.

Kumar, Narender. "Scheduled Castes in Transition". *Economic and Political Weekly.* Vol. XXXIV, No. 36. September 4, 1999.

Kumar, Raj. "Oriya Dalit Literature: A Historical Perspective". *The Fourth World: Journal of the Marginalized People.* No. 2. National Institute of Social Work and Social Sciences, Bhubaneshwar, October 1995.

——. "People at the Bottom: A Study of Untouchables in Indian Novels". *The Fourth World.* No. 8. NISSWASS, Bhubaneshwar: October 1998.

——. *Dalit Personal Narratives: Reading Caste, Nation and Identity.* New Delhi: Orient Blackswan, 2010.

Kumber, W.N. *Dr. Ambedkar: A Critical Study.* New Delhi: People's Publishing House, 1979.

Kunhappa, Murkot. *Sree Narayana Guru* (1982). New Delhi: National Book Trust, India, 1999.

Lieblich, Amia and Josselson, Ruthellen (eds). *Exploring Identity and Gender: The Narrative Study of Lives.* Thousand Oaks: Sage, 1994.

Limbale, Sharan Kumar. *Towards an Aesthetic of Dalit Literature: History, Controversies and Considerations.* Translated from the Marathi by Alok Mukherjee. Calcutta: Orient Longman, 2004.

Littrup, Lisbeth. *Identity in Asian Literature* (ed). Great Britain: Curzon Press, 1996.

Lohia, Ram Manohar. *The Caste System.* Hyderabad: Navahind, 1964.

Lucas, John (ed). *Writing and Radicalism.* New York: Longman, 1996.

Lutfullah. *Autobiography of Lutfullah: A Mohammedan Gentleman* (1854). Edited by Edward B. Eastwick. London: Smith, Elder and Co., 1863.

Malik, Bela. "Untouchability and Dalit Women's Oppression". *Economic and Political Weekly.* Vol. XXXIV. No. 6. February 6, 1999.

Man, Paul de. "Autobiography of De-facement". *Modern Literary Narrative.* Vol. 94. Johns Hopkins University: Johns Hopkins University Press, 1979.

Mane, Laxman. *Upara.* Translated as *Outsider* by A. K. Kamat. New Delhi: Sahitya Akademi, 1997.

Mani, Braj Ranjan. *Debrahmanising History: Dominance and Resistance in Indian Society.* New Delhi: Manohar, 2005.

Marathe, Sudharkar and Mukherjee, Meenakshi (eds). *Narrative: Forms and Transformations.* Delhi: Chanakya Publications, 1986.

Marcus, Laura. *Autobiographical Discourses: Theory, Criticism, Practice.* Manchester: Manchester University Press, 1994.

Martin, Luther M. *et al.* (eds) *Technology of the Self: A Seminar with M. Foucault.* Amherst, University of Massachusetts Press, 1988.

Mathew, Joseph. *Ideology, Protest and Social Mobility: Case Study of Mahars and Pulayas.* New Delhi: Inter-India Publications, 1986.

McDonald, Christie (ed). *The Ear of the Other: Autobiography, Transference, Translation.* Lincoln and London: University of Nebrska Press, 1988.

Mehta, Ved. *Face to Face: An Autobiography* (1957). Bombay: Jaico Publishing House, 1963.

Mec Leed, John. *Beginning Postcolonialism.* New Delhi: Viva, 2007.

Mendelsohn, Oliver and Vicziany, Marika. *The Untouchables: Subordination, Poverty and the State in Modern India.* New Delhi: Cambridge University Press, 2000.

Menon, K. P. S. *Many Worlds: An Autobiography* (1964). Bombay: Oxford University Press, 1966.

Menon, Ritu (ed). *Women Who Dared.* New Delhi: National Book Trust, 2002.

Mill, John Stuart. *Autobiography and Literary Essays.* Edited by John M. Robson. Canada: University of Toronto Press, 1981.

Mirza, Heidi Safia. *Black British Feminism: A Reader.* London: Routledge, 1997.

Mishra, Ram Bali. *Caste and Caste Conflict.* New Delhi: Commonwealth Publishers, 1989.

Mohanti, Prafulla. *Through Brown Eyes* (1985). New Delhi: Penguin Books, 1988.

Moon, Vasant (ed). *Dr Babasaheb Ambedkar Writings and Speeches.* Vols. 1—17. Bombay: Education Department, Government of Maharashtra, 1990-2002.

——. *Vasti* (1985). Translated into English as *Growing up Untouchable in India: A Dalit Autobiography* by Gail Omvedt. United States of America: Rowman and Littlefield Publishers, 2001.

Moorthy, A. Krishna. Dalit Movement in North Arcot District.http://vakindia.org/archives/Vikalp-Aug2005.pdf.

Moraes, Dom. *My Son's Father: An Autobiography* (1968). Delhi: Vikas Publications, 1971.

Morris, Desmond and Marsh, Peter. *Tribes.* London: Pyramid Books, 1988.

Mujahid, Abdul Malik. *Conversion to Islam: Untouchables' Strategy for Protest in India.* Pennsylvania: Anima Publications, 1989.

Mukherjee, Prabhati. *Beyond the Four Varnas: The Untouchables in India.* Simla: Indian Institute of Advanced Study, 1988.

Mukherjee, Ramakrishna. "Caste in Itself, Caste and Class, or Caste in Class". *Economic and Political Weekly.* Vol. XXXIV. No. 27. July 3, 1999.

Mukherjee, Sujit. *Autobiography of an Unknown Cricketer.* Delhi: Ravi Dayal Publisher, 1996.

Murthy, B. S. *Depressed and Oppressed.* New Delhi: S. Chand, 1971.

Murugkar, Lata. *Dalit Panthers Movement in Maharashtra: A Sociological Appraisal.* Bombay: Popular Prakashan, 1991.

Nagraj, D. R. *The Flaming Feet: A Study of Dalit Movement in India.* Bangalore: South Forum Press, 1993.

Naik, M. K. *et al. Critical Essays on Indian Writing in English.* Madras: Macmillan, 1977.

——. *A History of Indian English Literature.* New Delhi: Sahitya Academi, 1982

——. *Dimensions of Indian English Literature.* New Delhi: Sterling Publishers, 1985.

——. *A History of Indian English Literature.* New Delhi: Sahitya Akademi, 1989.

Nanda, Meera. *Breaking the Spell of Dharma.* New Delhi: Three Essays Press, 2002.

Narasimhaiah, C. D. and Srinath, C. N. *Bhakti in Indian Literature*. Mysore: Dhvanyoloka Publications, 1989.

Narayan, Badri and Misra, A. R. *Multiple Marginalities: An Anthology of Dalit Writings*. Delhi: Manohar, 2004.

Narayan, Jayaprakash. *Prison Diary: 1975*.Edited by A. B. Shah. Bombay: Popular Prakashan, 1977.

Nasrin, Taslima. *My Girlhood: An Autobiography*. Translated by Gopa Majumdar. New Delhi: Kali for Women, 2001.

Nehru, Jawaharlal. *An Autobiography* (1936). New Delhi: Oxford University Press, 1982.

Neuman, Shirley (ed). *Autobiography and Questions of Gender*. England: Frank Cass, 1991.

Nimbalkar, Waman. *Dalit Literature: Nature and Role*. Nagpur: Prabodhan Prakashan, 2006.

Olney, James. *Metaphors of Self: The Meaning of Autobiography*. Princeton: Princeton University Press, 1972.

——(ed). *Autobiography: Essays Theoretical and Critical*. Princeton: Princeton University Press, 1980.

——. *Studies in Autobiography*, New York: Oxford University Press, 1988.

Omvedt, Gail. *Cultural Revolt in a Colonial Society*. Bombay: Scientific Socialist Education Trust, 1976.

——(ed). *Land, Caste and Politics in Indian States*. New Delhi: Guild Publications, 1982.

——. *From Untouchable to Dalit: Essays on the Ambedkar Movement*. New Delhi: Manohar, 1992.

Omvedt, Gail. *Dalits and Democratic Revolution: Dr. Ambedkar and the Dalit Movement in Colonial India.* New Delhi: Sage, 1994.

——. "Towards a Theory of' Brahminic Patriarchy". *Economic and Political Weekly.* Vol. XXXV. No.4. January 22, 2000.

——. *Buddhism in India: Challenging Brahmanism and Caste.* New Delhi: Sage, 2003.

——. *Dalit Visions: The Anti-Caste Movement and the Construction of an Indian Identity.* New Delhi: Orient Longman, 2006.

Pandian, M. S. S. "'Denationalising' the Past: Nation in E. V. Ramaswamy's Political Discourse". *Economic and Political Weekly.* Vol. XXVIII. No. 42. October 16, 1993.

Pandit, Vijaya Lakshmi. *The Scope of Happiness: A Personal Memoir.* New Delhi: Vikas Publishing House, 1979.

Pannikkar, K. M. *An Autobiography.* Translation from the Malayalam by K. Krishnamurthy. Madras: Oxford University Press, 1977.

Paramhansa, Yogananda. *Autobiography of a Yogi.* London: Rider, 1963.

Parikh, Indira J. and Garg, Pulin K. *Indian Women: An Inner Dialogue.* New Delhi: Sage, 1989.

Pascal, Roy. *Design and Truth in Autobiography.* London: Routledge and Kegan Paul, 1960.

Patankar, Bharat and Omvedt, Gail. *The Dalit Liberation Movement in Colonial Period.* New Delhi: Critical Quest, 2007.

Pathy, Dinanath. *Drawing Master of Digapahandi.* Translated from Oriya by the author with Niranjan Mohanty. New Delhi: Harman Publishing House, 1995.

Patil, Sandeep. *Sandy Storm.* New Delhi: Rupa, 1984.

Pawar, Urmila. *Aaidan* (Marathi). Bombay: Granthali, 2003.

Pawde, Kumud. *Antasphot* (Marathi). Aurangabad: Anand Prakashan,1981.

Pecora, Vincent P. *Nations and Identities.* Great Britain: Blackwell, 2001.

Phule, Jotiba. *Collected Works of Mahatma Jotirao Phule.* Vols. I and II. Translated by P. G. Patil. Bombay: Education Department, Government of Maharashtra, 1991.

Pillai, G. K. *Origin and Development of Caste.* Allahabad: Kitab Mahal, 1959.

Pilling, John. *Autobiography and Imagination: Studies in Self-Scrutiny.* London: Routledge, 1981.

Potter, Jonathan *et al. Social Texts and Context: Literature and Social Psychology.* London: Routledge and Kegan Paul, 1984.

Prabash, J. *Social Change and Mobility through protest: Dalit Movements in the Erstwhile Princely State of Travancore, Kerala.* http://vakindia.org/archives/ Vikalp-Aug2005.pdf.

Prasad, Rajendra. *Autobiography* (1957). New Delhi: National Book Trust, 1994.

Prashad, Vijay. "Untouchable Freedom: A Critique of the Bourgeois-Landlord Indian State". *Subaltern Studies.* Vol. X. Delhi: Oxford University Press, 1999.

Price, Major David. *Memoirs of the Emperor Jahangir* (1928). New Delhi: Mittal Publications, 1985.

Pritam, Amrita. *The Revenue Stamp.* New Delhi: Vikas Publishing House, 1977.

Punalekar, S. P. "Experience, Perception and Reality: A Study of Dalit Literature in Maharashtra". Paper presented at a seminar organised by the Centre for Studies, Surat, February 1988.

Purushotham, K. 'Evolution of Telugu Dalit Literature', *Economic and Political Weekly*, Vol. XLV, No. 22, May, 2010.

Qasim, Mir. *My Life and Times.* New Delhi: Allied Publishers, 1992.

Rai, Lala Lajpat. *The Story of My Life: An Unknown Fragment.* Edited by Joginder Singh Dhanki. New Delhi: Gitanjali Prakashan, 1978.

Rajan, Rajeswari Sunder. *Real and Imagined Women: Gender, Culture and Post-colonialism.* London: Routledge, 1993.

Ram, Jagjivan. *Caste Challenge in India.* New Delhi: Vision Books, 1980.

Ram, Ronki. *Manguo Ram, Ad-Dharm and the Dalit Movement in Punjab.* New Delhi : Critical Quest, 2008.

Ramteke, D. L. *Revival of Buddhism in Modern India.* New Delhi: Deep and Deep Publications, 1983.

Ranade, Ramabai. *Amchya Ayushatil Kahi Athavani.* (1910). Translated as *Ranade: His Wife's Reminiscences* by Kusumavati Deshpande. New Delhi: Publications Division, Government of India, 1963.

Ranga, N. G. *Fight for Freedom: An Autobiography.* New Delhi: S. Chand and Co., 1968.

Rao, Anupama (ed). *Gender and Caste.* New Delhi: Kali for Women, 2003.

Rao, M. S. A. *Social Movements in India.* New Delhi: Manohar Publications, 1984.

Rao, R. Sangeetha. *Caste System in India: Myth and Reality:* New Delhi: India Publishers and Distributors, 1989.

——. "Static Society". *Ambedkar Medical Bulletin.* Vol. 27. No. 2. November-December, 1994.

Reed-Danahay, Deborah E. *Auto/Ethnography: Rewriting the Self and the Social.* Oxford: Berg, 1992.

Rege, Sharmila. *Writing Caste/Writing Gender: Narrating Dalit Women's Testimonies.* New Delhi: Zuban, 2006.

Louis, Prakash. *People Power: The Naxalite Movement in Central Bihar.* New Delhi : Wordsmiths, 2002.

——. *The Political Sociology of Dalit Assertion.* New Delhi: Gyan, 2003.

Rousseau, Jean Jacques. *Emile.* Translated by Barbara Foxley. Everyman: London, 1993.

Roy, M. N. *Memoirs.* Bombay: Allied Publishers, 1964.

Roy, Pascal. *Design and Truth in Autobiography,* London: Routledge and Kegal Paul, I960.

Roy, Ramashray. "The Concept of Development: Its Implications for Self and Society". *Psychology and Developing Societies.* Vol. 3, No. 2. New Delhi: Sage Publications, 1991.

——. *Self and Society: A Study in Gandhian Thought.* New Delhi: Sage, 1985.

Sagar, Sunder Lal. *Hindu Culture and Caste System in India.* Delhi: Uppal Book Store, 1975.

Sahgal, Lakshmi. *A Revolutionary Life: Memoirs of a Political Activist.* New Delhi: Kali for Women, 1997.

Sahgal, Nayantara. *Prison and Chocolate Cake.* London: Victor Gollanez, 1954.

——. *From Fear Set Free.* London: Victor Gollanez, 1962.

Saksena, S. P. (ed). *Indian Autobiographies.* Calcutta: Oxford University Press, 1949.

Sangari, Kum Kum and Vaid, Sudesh. *Recasting Women: Essays in Colonial History* (ed). New Delhi: Kali for Women, 1989.

Sangwan, Om Prakash. *Dalit Society and the Challenge of Development.* New Delhi: Commonwealth Publishers, 1996.

Sampurnanand. *Memories and Reflections.* Bombay: Asia Publishing House, 1962.

Saraswati, Dayanand. *Autobiography of Swami Dayanand Saraswati.* Edited by K. C. Yadav. Delhi: Manohar, 1976.

Saraswati, Pandita Ramabai. *The High Caste Hindu Woman.* Philadelphia: Pandita Ramabai, 1888.

——. *A Testimony of Our Inexhaustible Treasure.* Pune: Pandita Ramabai Mission, 1992.

Sarkar, Tanika. *Words to Win: The Making of Amar Jiban, A Modern Autobiography.* New Delhi: Kali for Women, 1999.

Satya Narayana, K. *Indian Writing in English; Course II.* Hyderabad: EFLU Publications, 2005.

Savarkar, S. D. *The Story of My Transportation for Life: A Biography of Black Days of Andamans.* Bombay: Sadbhakti Publications, 1950.

Scott, James C. *Weapons of the Weak: Everyday Forms of Peasant Resistance.* Delhi: Oxford University Press, 1990.

Seldon, Raman (ed). *A Render's Guide to Contemporary Literary Theory.* New Delhi: Pearson, 2007.

Senapati, Phakirmohana. *My Times and I.* Translated from Oriya by John Boulton. Bhubaneswar: Orissa Sahitya Akademi, 1985.

Seneviratne, H. L. *Identity, Consciousness and the Past: Forging of Caste and Community in India and Sri Lanka.* Delhi: Oxford University Press, 1997.

Sengupta, Arjun. "Debate on Discrimination: Casteism is Racism of another Sort" in *Caste, Race and Discrimination: Discourses in International Context,* Edited by Sukhadeo Thorat and Umakanth. New Delhi, Rawat Publications, 2004.

Sengupta, Padmini. *Pandita Ramabai Saraswati: Her Life and Work.* Bombay: Asia Publishing House, 1970.

Setalvad, Teesta. "Hidden Apartheid," in *Caste, Race and Discrimination: Discourses in International Context,* Edited by Sukhadeo Thorat and Umakanth. New Delhi, Rawat Publications, 2004.

Sharma, K. L. (ed). *Caste and Class in India.* Jaipur: Rawat Publications, 1994.

Sharma, Satish K. *Reform, Protest and Social Transformation.* New Delhi: Ashish Publishing House, 1987.

Shaw, Ghanshyam (ed). *Dalit Identity and Politics.* New Delhi: Sare, 2001.

Shyamlal. *Untold Story of a Bhangi Vice-Chancellor.* Jaipur: University Book House, 2001.

Singh, Balwant. *An Untouchable in the IAS*. Saharanpur: Prem Printing Press, 1997.

Singh, Khushwant. *Truth, Love and a Little Malice: An Autobiography*. New Delhi: Viking, 2002.

Singh, P. N. "Dalit: Dialectics of Myth and Reality". *Critique: A Journal of Critical Theory*. Vol. 2, No. 1. September, 1997.

Sinha, R. C. P. *The Indian Autobiographies in English*. New Delhi: S. Chand and Company, 1978.

Sivananda, Swami. *Autobiography of Swami Sivananda*. Tehri-Garhwal: Divine Life Society, 1983.

Smith, Anthony D. *Theories of Nationalism* (1971). London: Duckworth, 1983.

Smith, Sidonie and Watson, Julia (eds). *Decolonizing the Subject: Politics of Gender in Women's Autobiographies*. Minneapolis: University of Minnesota Press, 1991.

Smitha, Narula. "Caste Discrimination," in *Caste, Race and Discrimination: Discourses in International Context*, Edited by Sukhadeo Thorat and Umakanth. New Delhi, Rawat Publications, 2004.

Spivak, Gayatri. *The Other Worlds*. New York: Methun, 1987.

Srinivas, M.N. *Caste in Modern India and Other Essays*. Bombay: Asia Publishing House, 1962.

——. *The Dominant Caste and Other Essays*. Delhi: Oxford University Press, 1987.

Stone, Albert E. (ed). *The American Autobiography: A Collection of Criminal Essays*. New Jersey: Englewood Cliffs, 1981.

Subbamma, Malladi. *Fearless Feminist: An Autobiography of a Social Revolutionary*. Hyderabad: Booklinks, 1994.

Swaroopa Rani, Challapalli. "Dalit Women's Writing in Telugu," in *Economic and Political Weekly*, April 25, 1998.

——. "Dalit Feminist Literature and the influence of Ambedkar," in *Dalit Voice*. Hyderabad: Dalit Voice Publications, 2006.

Tagore, Rabindranath. *Reminiscences* (1917). Madras: Macmillan, 1987.

Thapar, Raj. *All These Years: A Memoir*. New Delhi: Seminar Publications, 1991.

Thapar, Romesh (ed). *Tribe, Caste and Religion in India*. Delhi, Macmillan, 1977.

Thapar, Romila. *The Past and Prejudice*. New Delhi: National Book Trust, 1993.

Tharakam, Bojja (ed). *The First All India Dalit Writers Conference: A Commemorative Volume*. Hyderabad: Dr B. R. Ambedkar Memorial Trust, 1994.

Thekaekara, Mari Marcel. "Annihilating Caste," in *Caste, Race and Discrimination: Discourses in International Context,* Edited by Sukhadeo Thorat and Umakanth. New Delhi, Rawat Publications, 2004.

Thorat, Sukhadeo and Umakanth (ed). *Caste, Race and Discrimination: Discourses in International Context*. New Delhi, Rawat Publications, 2004.

Tripathy, Rebati Bhallav. *Dalits: A Sub-Human Society*. New Delhi: Ashish Publishing House, 1994.

Venkataraman, R. *My Presidential Years*. New Delhi: Indus, 1995.

Verma, Vidhu. "Colonialism and Liberation: Ambedkar's Quest for Distributive Justice". *Economic and Political Weekly*. Vol. XXXIV, No. 39. September 25, 1999.

Vira, Dharam. *Reminiscences*. New Delhi: Vikas Publishing House, 1990.

Viswanathan, Gauri. *Outside the Fold: Conversion, Modernity, and Belief.* New Delhi: Oxford University Press, 1998.

Waghmare, Janardan. *The Quest for Black Identity.* Pune: Sugava Prakashan, 2001.

Webster, John C.B. *et al*. *From Role to Identity: Dalit Christian Women in Transition.* Delhi: ISPCK, 1997.

——. *The Dalit Christians: A History*. Delhi: ISPCK, 1996.

Wright, Richard. *Black Boy*. London: Picador, 1945.

Young, James O. *Black Writers of the Thirties.* Baton Rouge: Louisiana State University Press, 1973.

Zelliot, Eleanor. *From Untouchable to Dalit.* New Delhi: Manohar, 1992.

——. "Dr Ambedkar and the Empowerment of Women," in *Gender and Caste: Issues in Contemporary Indian Feminism,* (ed. by Anupama Rao). New Delhi: Women Unlimited and Kali for Women, 2006.

Index

T

U

V

W

SB 15040/128